no crumbs left

no crumbs left

RECIPES FOR EVERYDAY FOOD MADE MARVELOUS

TERI TURNER

WITH ANN VOLKWEIN

PHOTOGRAPHY BY TIM TURNER

HOUGHTON MIFFLIN HARCOURT
BOSTON   NEW YORK   2019

Copyright © 2019 by Teri Turner LLC

Photography copyright © 2019 by Tim Turner

Photography on pages 9, 14, 17, 221 copyright © Barb Levant Photo

Prop styling by Lorrie J

Library of Congress Cataloging-in-Publication Data

Names: Turner, Teri (Food blogger), author. | Turner, Tim (Photographer), photographer.

Title: No crumbs left : whole30 endorsed, recipes for everyday food made marvelous / Teri Turner ;
photography by Tim Turner.

Description: Boston : Houghton Mifflin Harcourt, 2019. | Includes index. |

Identifiers: LCCN 2018057176 (print) | LCCN 2018057419 (ebook) | ISBN 9781328558121 (ebook) |
ISBN 9781328557476 (pob) |

Subjects: LCSH: Cooking. | Cooking, American. | LCGFT: Cookbooks.

Classification: LCC TX714 (ebook) | LCC TX714 .T869 2019 (print) | DDC641.5—dc23

LC record available at https://lccn.loc.gov/2018057176

Book design by Jennifer K. Beal Davis

Printed in China

C&C 10 9 8 7 6 5 4 3 2 1

To my mother, you filled our lives with music, love, and laughter. You are my sunshine. This book is dedicated to you.

contents

salads 100

what's for dinner 132

acknowledgments

Thank you to Melissa Hartwig Urban for starting a movement that has changed so many people's lives. I am eternally grateful for the trust and faith that you have placed in me.

To my kids: My feed is an ode to you. You are everything to me. Mothering is my north, and nothing makes me happier than watching you soar. Patrick, thank you for telling me I needed to get a hobby when I was criticizing you about spending too much time on Instagram—turns out you were right. Lucy, you were part of the creation—from coming up with the perfect name, Nocrumbsleft, to taking the original pictures and creating the Facebook page. You continue to inspire me. I love that we did this together.

Roy, thank you for everything you did to bring this project to fruition, from recipe testing and creation to helping me steer the ship. Though my focus was on the book, my heart was always with you. Thanks for being my person. You are my home. I love you.

To my parents: You gave me enough love to last a lifetime. I certainly hit the parental jackpot. Thank you for believing in us. You gave me everything I need, except more time.

To my sisters: Paula, thank you for your thoughtful and critical eye in editing. Patty Sue, thank you for your recipes and inspiration in the kitchen. I know that Mom and Dad link us in the most beautiful way forever, and there are no two other people I would have rather shared my childhood with.

Zach, what a journey this has been, and I feel so lucky that we have gotten to share it together. I have infinite gratitude. You make it all fun and always find the best way with your anything-is-possible attitude. Here's to flying beyond our skis—thanks for taking the leap with me. You are the Magic Elixir that makes it all work.

Lucy K., thank you for being my compatriot in the kitchen for 25 years. Everything you do behind the scenes makes it all work so seamlessly. Who knew we would wind up here!

Rachel, I wouldn't be in this moment if not for you, four years ago, pushing me off the diving board and telling me I could do it. Thanks for always being there every step of the way.

Laurie, sisters by choice, thanks for loving me, supporting me, and going all in with me. You make a difference for me every day.

Joanna, thanks for showing up for me and loving me. You are a bright light.

Mariia, thank you for your dedication, energy, and intuitiveness.

Lori, thanks for holding down the fort with all the details to allow me to create.

Tim, what a wild ride. Thank you for selflessly and fully taking Nocrumbsleft on and teaching Zach and me from the start. This book was such a labor of love and you took it on as if it were your own. You were right: You do bleed Nocrumbsleft.

Lorri J., what a fantastic collaboration this was. You arrived just when we needed you, and the experience was a gift.

Ann, thanks for making the project so much fun on top of recipe testing, editing, and getting us to the finish line. You were the calm within the storm.

To my circle of 5: You know who you are, and I love you.

Meg McCabe, thank you for suggesting that I do Whole30. I would say it worked out just fine.

Michael at Symmetry Breakfast, thanks for talking me off the ledge and supporting me in every way possible.

Nom Nom Paleo, thanks for such amazing support and mentorship.

Brian and Alex, thank you for messaging me late one Sunday night and changing my life. I am forever grateful.

Thank you to Alycia Noe and my other secret recipe testers.

Yaena, thank you for your creative infusion and being my food muse and friend.

Justin Schwartz, my editor at Houghton, Mifflin Harcourt, thank you for making this possible.

Thank you to the entire team at HMH for the amazing effort.

To Lisa Grubka and Christy Fletcher at Fletcher and Co.: Thank you for believing in me with kindness and enthusiasm.

Band Mothers and Daughters: This book is a love letter to my mother. Special love to all of you. I wish she were here with us to enjoy this moment.

And to my followers: I'm pretty much speechless, but what I can say is thank you for indulging in, loving, and taking part in my food filled journey. I can't wait for what is to come.

foreword

Teri Turner is basically my Julia Child.

I know, that's a bold statement, but minus the whole "bringing French cuisine to America" thing, they have a lot in common. They're both quirky in the most endearing way. They both have an encyclopedic knowledge of cooking techniques. And they both turn everyday whole-food ingredients into flavorful masterpieces with humor, grace, and approachability.

The difference is, Teri has Instagram, and watching her prep, cook, and style is as magical as her famous elixirs. Her no-nonsense style transfixes me—I get the sense that she runs her kitchen with military precision, but her warmth, grace, and authenticity makes me feel capable and inspired. I want her to come to my house not to cook *for* me, but to cook *with* me. And then, there's her food....

The first No Crumbs Left recipe I ever made was the Sizzling Everyday Roasted Chicken Breasts from her Instagram feed. I looked at the ingredients and thought, "How did she get *this* famous from cooking chicken with just four ingredients?" But I trusted Teri and followed the recipe to the letter.

It was the best chicken of my life: Simple. Juicy. Delicious. At that point, I became the self-appointed President of the Teri Turner Fan Club, which is what entitles me to write this foreword.

Today, I'm delighted to share the Teri I've grown to know and love, both through my iPhone screen and in real life, with all of you. Her food is as delicious as it is beautiful. Her expert tips will save you time, energy, and stress in the kitchen. And even here, on the printed page, her warmth and devotion to her craft and her readers will shine through.

It's the next best thing to having Teri at your house, cooking with you . . . although I'm still not giving up on that dream.

As Julia would certainly say when digging into a plate of Teri's chicken, *Bon appétit!*

Melissa Hartwig Urban
Whole30 Co-founder

introduction

I have always embraced change and something new. I'm not afraid to try and fail, and I'm certainly not afraid to succeed.

A few years ago, my kids were nearly out of the house, and I was ready for my next chapter. I had an Instagram account with forty-four followers, where I posted dishes from my kitchen and travel photos for friends and family. My life took a radical turn when late one Sunday night, a message came from two young publishers of an online magazine asking me to write a food column. I replied, "I don't know how to write, but I sure do know how to talk about food!" Sometimes life changes slowly, imperceptibly; but occasionally, there is a moment—just one crashing moment—that changes everything.

The popularity of No Crumbs Left astounds me on a daily basis. One miracle after another got this train rolling, and when asked how I got here, I tell people, Frankly, I'm a gal who loves to eat. When I'm not eating, I'm thinking about what to cook next. This love of food and cooking has long been my mistress, guiding me through births and deaths, marriage and divorce, endings and new beginnings. It's been my guide, my joy, and the topic (be-sides my kids) that I talk about the most. Food is my love language, and I speak it with astounding fluency.

While my mother did have a few home-run dishes, in truth she found cooking to be a daily chore. Early on, I realized I didn't want her struggle to be mine. If cooking was inevitable, I was going to find a way to enjoy it. My mother would be thrilled, though not surprised, to find that I have taken one of the few aspects of her life that she wasn't absolutely passionate about and turned it into a thriving enterprise. The quick pace of life today, and all our modern conveniences, disconnect us from enjoying cooking in the way people once did. I consider it a loss. To roast a pork shoulder in the oven on low heat with just a few spices for eight hours and then pull out something unbelievably delicious—now, that is magic.

Getting people into the kitchen, *getting them excited* about cooking real food and willing to try new things, is what motivates me. There is something so vital about people reconnecting with real food. I am beyond thrilled that my natural affinity for something I love resonates so positively for others. This is what I know for sure: cooking is not just about cooking. Cooking real food will change your life and transform your soul. I've watched that transformation many times. It's the mantra that greets me each day when I wake up.

At the heart of this book, and my cooking, are Magic Elixirs, from Marinated Red Onions (page 30) to dressings and condiments to simple pan juices and Smoky Pepitas (page 44). One of my life's pleasures is uncovering those elements that transform food from ordinary to extraordinary. Not only does this book teach you how to make my Magic Elixirs, but I hope it will start you on a path to creating your own.

I wrote this book because people ask me all the time, "Can I come over and cook with you?" This book is a way to have me in your kitchen, guiding you through the process, along with you on your cooking journey. I'm going to ask you to embrace new foods, ideas, and cooking techniques. Use this book; write in it. I want you to learn from me, but don't be restricted by these rules. They are simply a framework for knowing how to cook. Once these recipes are a part of your kitchen, you'll be able to change them up and improvise. So be inspired by these recipes, but make them your own. You'll find that some of my recipes are very simple, and others will take you up a notch when you're ready to try something new. It's important to know that succeeding in the kitchen is all about possibly failing first.

Embrace your cooking journey by knowing where your food comes from. A great place to start is by meeting the farmers at your local farmers' market and engaging with your butcher, baker, and fishmonger. Get interested in cooking seasonally as a way of embracing the change of seasons, rather than fighting it. This book will point you in that direction. I'm not here to challenge people who serve asparagus in the fall, but why don't we eat seasonally? On every level, it's better: for your health, for the planet, and even for how your food tastes. This is a real-food cookbook, whether you are a novice or an experienced cook seeking inspiration and fabulous recipes. Invite your family into the kitchen to cook with you. It's never too soon or too late. It's been a joy to watch my kids grow up and begin to cook for themselves.

Sharing my passion with you has been a labor of love, an accumulation of my life's daily passion: cooking for my family and friends, for myself, and with my partner, Roy, the best cook I know.

Without further ado, I welcome you to my kitchen.

LET'S GO!

whole30

In February 2014, Roy and I decided to try Whole30.

Roy lasted twelve days. But I went all in, as I tend to do. I loved the way it made me feel and knew I was completely onto something. It transformed my cooking: if I could make really spectacular food that was gluten- and dairy-free, why wouldn't I want to all the time? A longtime advocate of natural foods, I enjoyed a clean-ish, gluten-free-ish diet, yet the Whole30 program elevated my energy, and my skin glowed like never before.

Resetting with Whole30 again and again has changed how I create and transform my favorite recipes into Whole30 and "Whole30-ish" dishes. My approach is to take old-school, seasonal, classic dishes and do my unique Whole30 spin on them. That unique spin includes my concept of Magic Elixirs, which are a perfect match for Whole30 cooking. Magic Elixirs are homemade concoctions that elevate food from ordinary to extraordinary. For me, it's not about lamenting the foods you can't eat but celebrating all the things you can—and the Magic Elixirs are what take food over the top. I love the idea of food as a celebration. Even when not doing a reset, I keep my kitchen Whole30 on weekdays, unless I'm traveling or attending events.

The Whole30 community is alive with the magic of passionate people supporting and empowering one another. After declining previous book offers that didn't feel quite right, nothing could have delighted me more than receiving an email from Melissa Hartwig Urban in September 2017, after my third @Whole30Recipes Instagram takeover, asking if I would create a Whole30-endorsed cookbook. I am forever grateful for the amazing grace I was extended when she invited me to write this cookbook.

pantry

Aleppo Pepper is less spicy than traditional red pepper flakes, and has an earthy and tangy flavor that makes it perfect to add a little kick to recipes.

Almond Meal is a Whole30 pantry necessity. It's perfect for making great dishes like a Whole30 chicken piccata or dredging a piece of fish or chicken.

Olive Oil is a Magic Elixir that I can't live without. Extra-virgin olive oil perfectly enhances the flavor of whatever you are cooking, and light olive oil is an essential ingredient in Whole30 mayonnaise.

Cassava Flour is a staple I always have in my pantry for Whole30 cooking. It's perfect for thickening sauces and soups or recipes that call for a delicate dusting for panfrying.

Chicken Stock is restorative, and a healing joy to make. It's also a must-have essential for making great soups and sauces. I know it seems like a hassle to make it homemade, but I want you to know it is going to make your cooking 100% better. See page 47!

Clarified Butter, made from grass-fed-cow milk, boasts a wonderful nutty flavor and caramelly sweetness that adds a delicious richness to whatever you are cooking. It's a must for Whole30 cooking. If you have never made it, homemade is so much more delicious than store-bought.

Coconut Milk is a nondairy alternative that thickens sauces, dressings, and soups and adds a delightful creaminess. Be sure to blend or stir all the more solid bits in the can into the rest of liquid before measure and using.

Coconut Oil is another staple for a complete Whole30 pantry. It is fabulous for sautéing and cooking foods at high heat.

Coconut Aminos add a great savory, slightly sweet flavor that I love in Asian-inspired stir-fries, marinades, dressings, and sauces. Think of it as a Whole30-compliant soy sauce.

Ginger (fresh) is second to none and brings a distinct flavor to dressings and marinades that is truly something special. Nothing beats fresh when it comes to ginger. See my juicing technique on page 296.

Herbs—sometimes you just need them! I like using both dried and fresh, but fresh often help your recipes pop with extra flavor and aroma.

Turmeric (fresh) is the perfect companion to ginger with its tangy and citrusy flavor, and it's easier to find than you'd think—look in the produce department at your grocery store. Worth seeking out! See my juicing technique on page 296.

Hearts of Palm are an essential for many of my "Teri Signature" salad platters. Their crunchy texture and mild flavor marry seamlessly with a savory vinaigrette or dressing.

Kosher Salt I love the flavor that it contributes to my cooking. I like Diamond Crystal kosher salt, but you may prefer sea salt— either is just fine, as it's all about personal preference.

Oregano (dried) is a delicious addition to marinades and spice rubs, and you can't make my Marinated Red Onions (page 30) without it, so it's something that is always in my pantry.

Pepperoncini, with their delicious tart-and-tangy flavor, do double-duty when you also cook with the great brine they're jarred in. A wonderful Magic Elixir to add to anything from a vinaigrette to chicken salad!

Pistachios are the key ingredient to one of my Magic Elixirs, Pistachio Pesto (page 51), to which they add a uniquely nutty sweetness— so I make sure I never run out!

Sumac (ground) is my go-to spice, and I use it in everything. Its flavor is bright, lemony, and slightly tart. I get mine at my local Middle Eastern store, but you can order it online.

Thai Chiles have a little more kick than a lot of peppers, but I love to use them in Asian-inspired cooking, so I always keep them on hand. I prefer fresh, but when you can't find them, you can rely on dried.

kitchen tools

A **Box Grater**, the old-fashioned kind, is my favorite. They're easy to use, simple to clean, and inexpensive.

An old-school **Cast-Iron Pan** is a must-have and will last you a lifetime—and then some. I'm lucky enough to have had one passed down to me, but it's easy to pick one up for yourself, as they're one of the most reasonably priced pans you will come across. Plus, it's all-purpose, an absolute workhorse, and goes from stovetop to oven and back. Never put a cast-iron pan in the dishwasher.

Cutting Boards that have a well around the edge are the best way to collect your meat juices—and you know I love those delectable meat juices, which can become the basis for some of your most exquisite Magic Elixirs. A cutting board is something you will have for life and use again and again, so invest in a good one.

An **Electric Slicer** is an absolute necessity for gluten-free or Whole30 cooking. This small kitchen appliance is going to make your life easier, from slicing your Marinated Red Onions to achieving perfect zucchini slices for grilling to creating uniformly sliced sweet potato crisps—and even cutting a Slow-Roasted Beef Eye of Round (page 184). Priced around $100, I've found that it has practically paid for itself.

A **Fish Turner** is perfect for keeping delicate fish intact.

A **Food Processor** is an essential tool in the kitchen and one you will have forever. The width of the bowl is perfect for certain jobs that can't be done with any other tool. I use mine for so many favorites, from Pistachio Pesto (page 51) to Lucy's Favorite Potato Pancakes (page 230), and all the attachments get plenty of use.

A **Garlic Press** is the perfect tool to make using fresh garlic easy. Get a high-quality, heavy-duty one, and it can last for years!

A **High-Speed Blender** will help you make velvety blended soups, turn out perfectly textured nut butters, and crush ice for beverages. Recipes that call for combining food

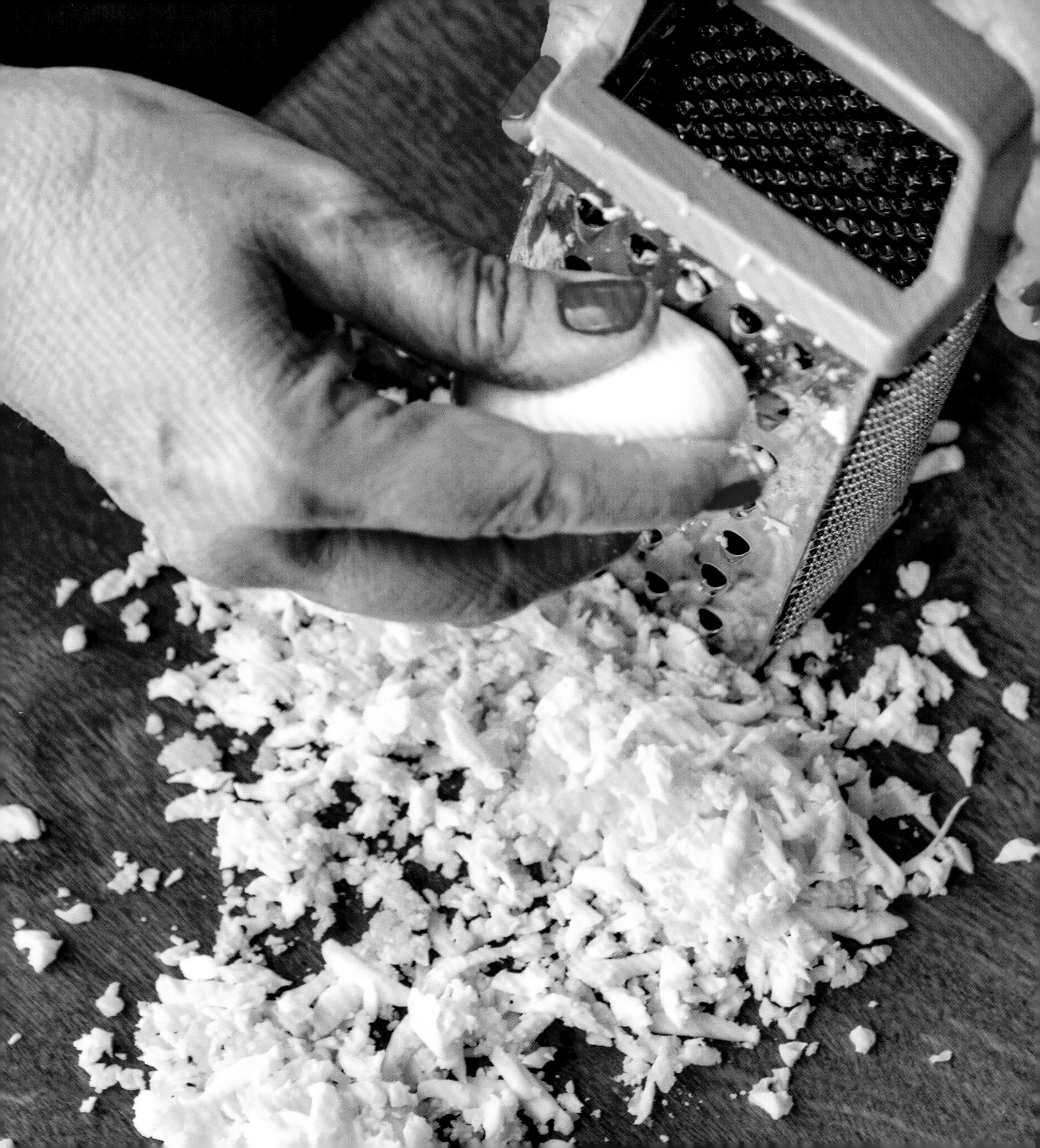

like smoothies or soups with frozen fruit and vegetables, whether hot or cold, will be easier with a high-speed blender. I found my first one at a secondhand store! It was gently loved, and I went on to use it for twenty more years. They are a bit of an investment, but well worth it. Think of it as a lifetime appliance.

An **Immersion Blender**, what a useful tool! I love mine for Whole30 cooking and use it daily for most of my sauces, including mayo and salad dressings. I consider it a must-have, and all things considered, you can get one for a very reasonable price.

A **Kitchen Scale** is a must! You'll want to weigh patties for chicken burgers or salmon cakes, and for baking, it's absolutely the way to go.

Knives are my favorite wedding gift to give. My favorite knives (those I consider essential) are a large paring knife, a chef's knife, a bread knife or other serrated knife, a carving knife,

and kitchen shears. Frankly, that's all you need; buying a full block of knives you may never use is unnecessary. Loving your knives makes cooking a pleasure. Keep them well sharpened.

Tongs are an essential tool for sautéing vegetables, flipping meat, or moving larger ingredients around in a pan.

A **Wooden Spoon** feels so natural to me. It won't damage your pans and will develop a beautiful patina over the years. Never put it in the dishwasher.

magic elixirs

I've always had a magic potion or two up my sleeve. A Magic Elixir is a genius combination of ingredients with a depth of flavor that elevates food from ordinary to extraordinary. They are a great way to streamline meal prep. My refrigerator is jammed full of Magic Elixirs—some I cook up, and some are naturally occurring. A cook with Magic Elixirs on hand will never feel deprived, and that is why they are the cornerstone of this book. I guarantee you'll be thrilled with everyday eating if you keep jars of magically delicious sauces, dressings, pesto, stocks, and other homemade flavor enhancers in your kitchen. It is not at all an exaggeration to say that people have been moved to tears when eating a sandwich topped with one or more of my special sauces. All the Magic Elixirs in this chapter happen to be Whole30.

marinated red onions

Daily love letters arrive from people I've never met, all because of a little bowl of marinated red onions, or "counter onions," as we call them, that my family has enjoyed over the years. Only when I posted them on Instagram did I realize that others would embrace them as much as we had. In my kitchen, this game-changing Magic Elixir has been a special sauce that turns almost any ordinary dish into an extraordinary one. I continue to be delighted by how wildly loved they are. Followers from around the globe have kids who love them, and people who previously raised their hands as confirmed onion haters are now fans. They've even been kind of a gateway into the kitchen for many reluctant cooks. The messages and videos I receive from people raving about the difference marinated red onions have made in their life astound me—some even tell me that the little bowl of onions started them on a healthier path. Are you ready to make a batch?

Your onions will stay fresh for two to three days on the countertop. No need to put them in the refrigerator, because when the oil solidifies, the magic is gone. The oil itself is delicious on its own as a salad dressing, and any leftover onions can be sautéed up into crispy bits of sweet deliciousness. The simplicity of this dish makes it something anyone can make, and nothing makes me happier than to have people realize that they can learn to rule their own kitchens. See opposite for some great pairings.

MAKES 1¼ CUPS • COOK TIME: 5 MINUTES, PLUS 12 HOURS MARINATING TIME

Put the onion in a small, shallow bowl.

In a separate small bowl, mix the olive oil, vinegar, and oregano together until combined well. Pour the mixture over the onions. The marinade should completely cover the onions; if any are peeking out, then you have too many in the bowl.

Cover and let the onions marinate on the counter for at least 12 hours before using. They will keep for up to 3 days. Do not refrigerate. (But you may refrigerate the oil after the onions are gone!).

"An apron is just a cape on backwards."
—Unknown

1 small, ½ medium, or ¼ large red onion, thinly sliced into rounds

¾ cup extra-virgin olive oil

1 tablespoon red wine vinegar

1 tablespoon dried oregano

TERI'S TIPS
After the onions are gone, don't throw away the oil! Refrigerate it to use as the base for a salad dressing or a marinade.

PAIRS WITH . . .

Any salad, including Italian Chopped Salad (page 120), Lamb Chop Salad (page 114), Steak Lemon Caesar (page 117), Chicken Finger Salad (page 109), Tropical Cobb (page 106), Slow-Roasted Beef Salad (page 118), and anything and everything that is edible.

garlic confit

GLUTEN-FREE
DAIRY-FREE
WHOLE30
PALEO
GRAIN-FREE

Though people have been making garlic confit for ages, Gjelina, an LA restaurant, certainly brought it to the forefront. That's where I first tried it, and I've been making my own version ever since. I cook the garlic slowly in oil to give it an almost buttery consistency. As essential to my pantry as salt and black pepper, the tenderness and gentle taste will make this a staple for you, too. You can change this up by using any of your favorite fresh herbs. MAKES ABOUT 3 PINTS • COOK TIME: 35 MINUTES

4   cups peeled garlic cloves

3   cups extra-virgin olive oil

½   cup fresh basil leaves

2   sprigs rosemary

2   bay leaves

"There is no such thing as 'a little garlic.'"   —Unknown

Preheat the oven to 350°F.

In a medium baking pan with sides, spread the garlic out evenly. Pour the olive oil over, making sure the garlic is completely covered with the oil. Tuck in the basil, rosemary, and bay leaves, and bake for 35 minutes, or until the garlic is lightly browned and soft.

Remove from the oven and let cool to room temperature. Once cooled, transfer the garlic confit to glass jars, making sure the oil is covering the garlic, and seal the jars. Store in the refrigerator for up to 6 weeks.

PAIRS WITH . . .
Grapefruit-Lime Vinaigrette (page 58), Zucchini Pie (page 72), Broccolini Chicken Breakfast Hash (page 77); add it to a soup or a stir-fry, a frittata, a bowl of my Plant-Based Chili (page 249) or P. S.'s Chili (page 239), or to Cashew Crema (page 65) to make a garlic cream sauce, or anywhere you want a gentle garlic flavor; serve it with eggs, blend it into a sauce, use it to top a steak; drizzle the oil on top of cooked vegetables or cauliflower rice.

TERI'S TIPS
Chefs have been using the "confit" method (slowly cooking in fat) for ages. I love to confit everything from turkey legs to garlic, tomatoes and onions. To confit something is to create one of the best Magic Elixirs of all time.

tomato confit

GLUTEN-FREE
DAIRY-FREE
WHOLE30
PALEO
GRAIN-FREE

I'm going to let you in on a little secret: I've found a way to get a bit of sunshine all winter long. Having a jar of tomato confit available year-round allows me to add the taste of summer to almost any dish, anytime. I always double this recipe, because it's the same amount of work to do twice as much. It's perfect to share or to give as a hostess gift. I use it whenever I want an infused tomato flavor: in a soup or soup base, in a salad dressing, as a condiment; mixed with mayo, guacamole, or Cashew Crema (page 65); or blended as a homemade ketchup. Gjelina, a restaurant in LA, ignited my love for tomato confit, and my spin on this classic recipe and kitchen staple easily brings out the best of what a tomato already has to offer. It's the secret weapon you never knew you needed. MAKES ABOUT 3 PINTS • COOK TIME: 30 MINUTES

5	cups cherry tomatoes
2½	cups extra-virgin olive oil
1	cup fresh basil leaves
2	garlic cloves, crushed
1	teaspoon kosher salt

Preheat the oven to 350°F.

In a shallow baking dish (11 × 7-inch works well), immerse the tomatoes in the olive oil, ensuring that the tomatoes are completely covered. Tuck the basil leaves and garlic into the dish and sprinkle with the salt. Bake for 30 minutes, or until the tomatoes are tender, hot, and bubbling.

Remove from the oven and let cool to room temperature. Once cooled, transfer the tomatoes and oil to glass jars, making sure the oil completely covers the tomatoes, and seal the jars. Store in the refrigerator for up to 1 month.

VARIATIONS

Spicy: Add 1 teaspoon each of hot paprika and smoked paprika, and swap 1 sliced red Fresno pepper for the garlic and basil.

Balsamic: Blend ½ cup Tomato Confit with the oil, 1 tablespoon balsamic vinegar, and 1/8 teaspoon kosher salt until smooth.

gomasio

Gomasio is a delicious flavored salt made from roasted sesame seeds and sea salt. I used to buy it from my friend Nancy, who had a small company, but when she went out of business I was compelled to create my own. Gomasio makes every recipe better. Along with my Marinated Red Onions (page 30), this is a mainstay on my kitchen counter. Members of my family can be found standing over the bowl, eating directly from it. Gomasio's nutty, salty flavor is so good sprinkled on just about everything, from eggs to salads to vegetables. It's easy to make, but be sure to buy fresh sesame seeds, as they are a must!

MAKES ABOUT ½ CUP • COOK TIME: 8 MINUTES

Heat a medium skillet over medium heat. Add the white and black sesame seeds and salt and stir to combine. Cook, stirring continuously, until the seeds are toasted, 2 to 3 minutes; if they begin to burn, reduce the heat to medium-low. Immediately transfer half the toasted seeds to a bowl; pour the remainder into a mortar and smash them with the pestle until ground, about 4 minutes.

Transfer the ground seeds to the bowl with the whole seeds and stir to combine. Cool and store in an airtight container for up to 8 weeks.

¼ cup raw white sesame seeds

¼ cup raw black sesame seeds

1½ teaspoons Himalayan pink salt

VARIATION

Feel free to mix it up and make this gomasio your own. I love adding ½ teaspoon granulated garlic and ½ teaspoon smoked paprika to the bowl after toasting the seeds.

PAIRS WITH . . .

Pot Sticker Fish Cakes (page 210), Sweet-and-Sour Fish (page 205), Zucchini Ribbons with Ginger Marinade (page 264), and Patrick's Vegetarian Feast (page 269).

preserved meyer lemons

Oh so simple to make, and a true Magic Elixir, preserved lemons have been enjoyed for over a thousand years, probably because they are the ideal flavor-enhancing addition to so many dishes. A little goes a long way, so start with one piece of preserved lemon and add more gradually, until your recipe tastes just the way you want it to. MAKES 1 QUART • COOK TIME: 5 MINUTES, PLUS 3 DAYS MARINATING TIME

Pour 2 cups of the salt into a small baking dish, spreading it out into an even layer. Roll the lemon wedges in the salt until thoroughly coated.

Put the remaining 2 tablespoons salt in the bottom of a 1-quart mason jar. Add the lemons to the jar, pushing down and pressing them with a wooden spoon or muddler until they're largely squeezed and covered with their own juice. If need be, take a few of them out and squeeze their juices out on top of the others. The lemons must be completely submerged in juice, but there also must be a bit of room at the top of the jar to allow the lemons to expand as they soak. Top the lemons with the olive oil and screw on the lid. Keep them on the counter for 3 days, gently shaking the jar once a day, then transfer to the refrigerator. They will keep for up to 6 months.

To use, remove some lemons from the jar, finely chop them, and press the pieces through a garlic press. (This makes a mess!) Add to anything you like when you're looking for a salty, lemony, briny seasoning.

"Often I will start with one of my trusted recipes, then I open my box of tricks and add sauces, oils, powders, and garnishes, as a child might experiment with building blocks." —Jean-Christophe Novelli

2 cups plus 2 tablespoons kosher salt

4 Meyer lemons, each cut into 8 wedges

2 tablespoons extra-virgin olive oil

PAIRS WITH . . .
Lemon Caesar Dressing (page 56); mix it with Marinated Red Onion oil (page 30) to make a delicious dressing, or with Whole30 Mayonnaise (page 286) to create a wonderful lemon-infused mayo; delicious in tuna salad, mixed with Pistachio Pesto (page 51), or simply on top of vegetables; add it to Garlic Confit (page 33) and spread the mixture over a salmon fillet before cooking.

TERI'S TIPS

Make sure to cut the lemons quite small so they can easily fit in the garlic press when you're ready to use them.

Preserved lemons are very salty; if you're adding them to a recipe that calls for salt, exclude it.

There will be leftover salt when you're done rolling. Save it to use in other recipes.

If the lemons aren't covered with lemon juice, they go bad.

You can make these with other types of lemon, but it's worth waiting for Meyers. I always double this recipe, but when I have Meyer lemons, I make enough for 6 months or more.

teri's 48 tips

1. Step away from the meat! Leaving meat to rest is an essential key to cooking. Everyone needs a cutting board with a well around the edge to catch the juices for a Magic Elixir.

2. Always save your cooking juices, from seafood to steak to chicken to pork. Catch them in the pan and collect them from your cutting board to incorporate into the dish you're making or to use as a Magic Elixir in a soup, a sauce, or as a finisher on another day.

3. Whenever you use coconut milk, blend it before measuring. Canned coconut milk separates into coconut cream and water.

4. A simple way to have a taste of summer all year round? Oven-dry a batch of cherry tomatoes when they're at their best. Just cut each tomato in half, put them on a baking sheet, and bake at 200°F until dry.

5. Old Bay Seasoning is a revelation.

6. When roasting chicken breasts, always do skin-on and bone-in. Spoon the pan drippings over the chicken toward the end; basting with the chicken fat makes the meat so much more delicious, and isn't that what life is all about?

7. As a rule of thumb, when baking a whole chicken, think 20 minutes per pound. When the leg and wing wiggle loosely, the chicken is done roasting.

8. Mason jars are my preferred refrigerator storage system. Did you know that you can freeze food in widemouthed pint-size Ball mason jars because the glass is tempered? Remember to only fill jars to 70 percent full before freezing; foods and liquids expand as they freeze, and you don't want the jar to shatter. Whether you're refrigerating or freezing them, always label your jars with the date and contents.

9. Freeze chicken stock in ice cube trays or widemouthed pint-size Ball mason jars (must be tempered glass). A cube of chicken stock can be helpful in a pan when everything's sticking, as it adds moisture and flavor without adding more oil.

10. Soaking dried mushrooms in hot water makes a lovely broth.

11. Ask your fishmonger to help with prep work—filleting the fish, deveining the shrimp, cooking and cracking the lobster. It's a skilled trade.

12. Cooking shrimp with the shell on is simply more delicious. It's possible to devein the shrimp and keep the shell on: Insert the tip of your kitchen shears just under the shell on the shrimp's back, where the head was, and gently cut through the shell (not the shrimp meat) down to the base of the tail, then remove the vein with your fingers, leaving the tail intact.

13. A salad is not a swimming pool. Don't drown it in dressing.
14. Fresh basil belongs on the counter, not in your refrigerator.
15. Many vegetables and herbs are like flowers and can be revived with a water bath.
16. When you're cooking, always set both a timer and a stopwatch. The timer tracks the individual elements and the stopwatch shows the entire process.
17. Use your hands! They are the best tool in your kitchen.
18. Touch your produce. It's important to be connected to the process.
19. Folks like your butcher, your farmer, and your fishmonger are the original passionate foodies and have so much to teach. Know their names, ask questions, and find out where your food comes from.
20. Don't be afraid to season your food; salt is your friend.
21. Change up your dried herbs and your spice profile regularly. Clean out your spice cabinet, and notice the expiration dates. Fresh spices make all the difference in the world. Expand your repertoire.
22. Add garlic toward the end of cooking; otherwise, it will burn and taste bitter.
23. When making a stir-fry, vegetable medley, or stew, I often cook each element one at a time, set them aside, then combine them just before serving. Each ingredient will be cooked perfectly. Takes a bit more time, but believe me, it's worth it.
24. I love ginger, just not too much. Grate fresh, unpeeled ginger until you have about ¼ cup. Squeeze the juice into a bowl and discard the pulp. Use the juice in a recipe to add a gentle ginger flavor, rather than overwhelming the entire dish. Do the same with turmeric (see page 296).
25. You will have a happier life if you find joy in the kitchen. (That's also true in the bedroom.)
26. When scrambling eggs, first blend them to get rid of striations, then cook them slow and low, moving them around often, for a magnificent, creamy result.
27. To get lovely, crispy potatoes, cook them twice: parboil them, then fry, bake, or roast.
28. You want a great, crispy potato, my friend? Use duck fat.
29. Blanching vegetables like green beans, sugar snap peas, and asparagus, then immediately placing them in an ice water bath to cool helps keep their vibrant color (see page 296).
30. Make a shrimp or shellfish stock with the shells and a few vegetables tossed in. It cooks in only 20 minutes, unlike a chicken stock, which can take all day.
31. In the spirit of tip-to-tail cooking, save all poultry carcasses to make stocks or bone broth. In addition, you can make a sublime stock reduction.
32. Don't even think about throwing out the oil from Marinated Red Onions (page 30)! Refrigerate it to use as the base for a salad dressing or a marinade.

continued...

33. Pair arugula with your breakfast to get your greens in. It's a great way to start almost any plate.

34. Always salt your salad greens.

35. Cloth napkins make food taste better. It's that simple.

36. To keep parsley and cilantro fresh, store them in a mason jar filled with an inch of water in the refrigerator. Do the same with asparagus; just trim off the ends first.

37. Gently warm plates in the oven on the lowest possible setting. Don't serve hot food on a cold plate.

38. For a fantastic steak, I use the 10:10:10 rule. For a 2¼-inch-thick steak on the bone, that's 10 minutes on the stove in a very hot pan, 10 minutes in a very hot oven, and 10 minutes resting. Vary the number of minutes according to your doneness preference and steak thickness. This ratio is just your jumping-off point.

39. Hand-grate hard-boiled eggs on the large holes of a box grater for the best egg salad.

40. Always get one extra of whatever you're going to fry. Maybe you've heard the advice, "Ruin the first pancake." It's necessary not just for pancakes, but also pork chops, eggplant Parmesan, chicken fingers, calamari—fry one first. Ruin it. Adjust time or temperature. Move forward. You get the picture.

41. Use the water from cooking vegetables to water your plants. Waste not, want not.

42. Challenge yourself to create something new all the time. Bring home items like ramps, garlic scapes, or Chinese broccoli. Embrace new items . . . and throw caution to the wind.

43. When a recipe calls for crushed tomatoes, buy canned whole tomatoes and crush them yourself. Manufacturers will leave the better tomatoes whole, and crush the not-so-great ones.

44. Write in your cookbooks. Pen marks and spills are welcome. This is the kind of behavior I encourage. It becomes part of your history.

45. If you have good silver and china, use it regularly. Better to break it than leave it in the cupboard and never use it.

46. It's okay to fail in the kitchen. Don't let that stop you. It's part of becoming an excellent cook.

47. Recipes are great, but sometimes it's fun to follow your intuition.

48. Cook from your heart. You will taste the difference.

smoky pepitas

These divine seeds are kind of a revelation. Smoky pepitas add a distinctly marvelous, spicy crunch to salads, soups, eggs, and practically anything else you can imagine. They are also a fantastic snack and nice to tuck into a lunchbox. Your kitchen will smell amazing when you make them. MAKES ½ CUP • COOK TIME: 5 MINUTES

In a small bowl, stir together the salt, smoked paprika, and granulated garlic until combined well. Set aside.

In medium stainless steel sauté pan, heat the olive oil over medium to medium-high heat. Add the pepitas and cook, stirring continuously, until browned, 4 to 5 minutes; watch them closely—if they char a little or start to burn, it's okay, just turn the heat down to low. Turn off the heat and add the spice mixture to the pepitas, stirring to coat well. Cool and store in an airtight container for up to 8 weeks.

"Something magical happens when food is cooking—the rest of the world melts away, and nothing exists except what's in the skillet in front of you—and it talks, breathes, and lives. The sounds, aromas, textures, flavors, and the heat of the kitchen—even the occasional searing burn—feel good."
—Donald Link

½	teaspoon kosher salt
½	teaspoon smoked paprika
½	teaspoon granulated garlic
1	teaspoon extra-virgin olive oil
½	cup raw hulled pepitas (pumpkin seeds)

TERI'S TIPS

There's a textural difference between granulated garlic and garlic powder, and I think the grainier granulated garlic is so much better.

PAIRS WITH . . .

Sugar Snap Pea and Smoky Pepita Salad (page 123) and Jerusalem Salad (page 131).

PAIRS WITH . . .

Shrimp Coconut Bowl (page 89), Portuguese Stew (page 87), Whole30 Vegetable Soup (page 84), Chicken Fricassee (page 164), Minestrone (page 232), Southeast Asian Curry Chicken (page156), Pork Chops and Parsnip Puree (page 141), Mediterranean Chicken Artichoke Stew (page 163), Spicy Shrimp on Creamy Smashed Potatoes (page 196), Citrus Cod with Sautéed Spinach (page 203), Lucja's Stuffed Cabbage (page 173), Roy's Salami and Cheddar Baked Rice (page 187), and Golden Onion Sauce (page 61).

chicken stock

GLUTEN-FREE
DAIRY-FREE
WHOLE30
PALEO
GRAIN-FREE

A good chicken stock is the heart, soul, and foundation of many recipes, and let me tell you, this one is excellent. Making your own stock adds a richness to your cooking that is second to none. Though making your own will take more time than just buying it from the store, it can be prepared ahead and frozen for later use. This is the kind of thing you will certainly want to have on hand at all times. Once you start making your own, it will become essential to your repertoire. MAKES ABOUT 9 CUPS • COOK TIME: UP TO 3½ HOURS (BUT AS LITTLE AS 1½ HOURS IF NECESSARY)

1   whole chicken
6   chicken backs (optional)
6   chicken wings (12, if not using backs)
    Chicken feet (optional)
2   tablespoons kosher salt
1   tablespoon whole black peppercorns
1   large white or yellow onion
5   medium carrots
5   medium celery stalks
½   medium celery root, peeled
1   medium parsnip
½   bunch flat-leaf parsley

TERI'S TIPS

Every week, I roast a butterflied chicken, which leaves me with a good supply of backs for stock. I also freeze the carcass once the meat is gone and use that for making stock, too.

If you wish, wash the chicken well and set it aside to dry. Cut the whole chicken into 9 pieces: wings, thighs, legs, breasts, and back. If you're using the additional backs, they need to be rinsed well and cleaned of anything you don't want in the stock.

Fill a large stockpot with 12 cups of water, leaving plenty of room for the ingredients. Bring the water to a boil. Add the salt and peppercorns.

Char the onion on the stove burner for 1 to 2 minutes, turning it with tongs to char all sides, and add it to the pot. Add all the chicken pieces (except the breasts), the carrots, celery, celery root, parsnip, and parsley and bring the water back to a boil. You will notice some white matter collecting on top; skim that off and reduce the heat to maintain a gentle simmer. Simmer slowly for 3 hours (ideally; but for at least 45 minutes). Taste the stock along the way and see how it changes. About 25 minutes before the end of the cooking time, add the chicken breasts.

Strain the stock, reserving the meat and discarding the other solids, and use immediately or let cool, then transfer to airtight containers and store in the refrigerator for up to 4 days or in the freezer. Use the reserved chicken breasts in Chicken Salad (page 97), Tropical Cobb (page 106), chili, or soup, or shred the meat and mix it with spices for a taco filling.

stir-fry infuser

GLUTEN-FREE
DAIRY-FREE
WHOLE30
PALEO
GRAIN-FREE

This is a delicious basic marinade for beef or chicken. A spoonful or two will infuse any simple stir-fry with that extra oomph. It's also good as an East Asian–style dipping sauce. MAKES ABOUT ¾ CUP • COOK TIME: 10 MINUTES

½   cup plus 1 tablespoon coconut aminos

¼   cup plus 2 tablespoons rice vinegar

1   tablespoon hot sauce (check label for compliance if doing Whole30)

    Juice from 3 tablespoons grated fresh ginger (see page 296)

1   teaspoon minced garlic

In a medium bowl, mix the coconut aminos, vinegar, hot sauce, ginger juice, and garlic until thoroughly combined. Serve or store in an airtight container in the refrigerator for up to 1 week.

> **PAIRS WITH . . .**
> Asian Steak Salad (page 115) and Shrimp Pad Thai (page 119); great as a light dipping sauce.

dipping sauce

MAKES ABOUT 1 CUP • COOK TIME: 5 MINUTES

½   cup coconut aminos

¼   cup plus 2 tablespoons rice vinegar

    Juice from 3 tablespoons grated fresh ginger (see page 296)

1   tablespoon hot sauce (check label for Whole30 compliance)

In a small bowl, stir together the coconut aminos, rice vinegar, ginger juice, and hot sauce. Serve or store in an airtight container in the refrigerator for up to 1 week.

pistachio pesto

GLUTEN-FREE
DAIRY-FREE
WHOLE30
PALEO
GRAIN-FREE

I have a confession: I am not a fan of basil pesto—it's too intense. When I developed this gentler, sweeter pistachio pesto, it quickly became a staple in my kitchen. I always have a jar on hand, because the nutty sweetness I just can't get enough of is perfect on almost everything—eggs, fish, chicken salad, or a dollop in a soup. Add it to meat loaf, stuff it into a burger—it's absolutely out of this world, and a bit of a game-changer. Nirvana. MAKES 1½ CUPS • COOK TIME: 10 MINUTES

1   cup shelled raw pistachios

1   cup fresh basil leaves

1   cup fresh flat-leaf parsley
    leaves

3   garlic cloves, pressed

½   cup extra-virgin olive oil

3   tablespoons fresh lemon juice

1   teaspoon kosher salt

½   teaspoon freshly ground
    black pepper

In a food processor, pulse the raw pistachios until coarsely chopped. Add the basil, parsley, and garlic and pulse until mixed well.

With the motor running, slowly add the olive oil, about one-third at a time, and process until combined well. Add the lemon juice, salt, and pepper and pulse until combined well.

Serve immediately or store in an airtight container in the refrigerator for up to 2 weeks.

> **PAIRS WITH . . .**
> Pistachio Pesto Chicken Breasts (page 143) and Whole30 Vegetable Soup (page 84); amazing in Teri's Favorite Chicken Salad (page 97) or Spring Breakfast (page 71), on top of Zucchini Pie (page 72), or mixed into Whole30 Mayonnaise (page 286) for an amazing dressing; serve it as a tasty condiment with roast chicken, pork, or lamb.

"Simple ingredients prepared in a simple way—that's the best way to take your everyday cooking to a higher level."
                                                            —José Andrés

999 island dressing

Here is my spin on a Thousand Island dressing that is pure bliss, and sure to impress. It's the result of my ongoing desire to create delicious and totally Whole30-compliant dressings and sauces. It's fantastic with a Crab Louie salad, or even just as a dipping sauce for seafood. This is truly a case where less is more. MAKES 1⅔ CUPS • COOK TIME: 15 MINUTES

In a food processor, combine the mayonnaise, tomato confit and oil, coconut aminos, hot sauce, tomato paste, garlic, salt, cayenne, and black pepper and process until smooth.

Transfer the mixture to a medium bowl. Add the cornichons, egg, and onions and stir until combined well.

Serve immediately or store in an airtight container in the refrigerator for up to 4 days.

> **PAIRS WITH . . .**
> Seafood Salad (page 129), Cassava-Crusted Calamari (page 222), Patrick's Chicken Fingers (page 251), Slow-Roasted Beef Eye of Round (page 184), and any seafood or vegetables.

¾ cup Whole30 Mayonnaise (page 286)

⅔ cup Tomato Confit (page 35), including some of the oil

2 tablespoons coconut aminos

1 tablespoon hot sauce (check label for compliance if doing Whole30)

1 tablespoon tomato paste

1 garlic clove, pressed

1 teaspoon kosher salt

½ teaspoon cayenne pepper

¼ teaspoon freshly ground black pepper

¼ cup finely chopped cornichons

1 large hard-boiled egg, grated

1½ tablespoons finely chopped white onion

green goddess dressing

My spin on the standard Green Goddess dressing is creamy, tangy, zesty, and, incidentally, healthful. It's great as a salad dressing or a dip. Get over yourself about the anchovies—they tie the dressing together, giving it a depth of flavor, and make it fantastic. If you love it as much as I do, you'll be making it twice a week! MAKES 1½ CUPS • COOK TIME: 10 MINUTES

In a food processor, combine the mayonnaise, olive oil, basil, tarragon, parsley, lemon juice, vinegar, anchovies, garlic, and salt and process until thoroughly combined. Taste and season with pepper and more salt and lemon juice, if needed.

Use immediately or store in an airtight container in the refrigerator for up to 6 days.

1 cup Whole30 Mayonnaise (page 286, see Tip)

¼ cup plus 1 tablespoon extra-virgin olive oil

¾ cup fresh basil leaves

¼ cup fresh tarragon leaves

¼ cup fresh parsley leaves

3 tablespoons fresh lemon juice, plus more if needed

2 tablespoons red wine vinegar

3 oil-packed anchovy fillets

3 garlic cloves, finely chopped

⅛ teaspoon kosher salt, plus more if needed

Freshly ground black pepper

PAIRS WITH . . .
Sugar Snap Pea and Smoky Pepita Salad (page 123), Lucy's Favorite Potato Pancakes (page 230), Green Beans Almondine (page 266), or vegetables; mix it with Tomato Confit (page 35) to make a tangy, sweet salad dressing; use the dip variation for crudités and sliced fresh tomatoes.

TERI'S TIPS
I always make this with freshly made Whole30 Mayonnaise (page 286). It's delicious, cheaper, and tastes better than store-bought. Homemade mayo is a bit different every time you make a batch. Take the time to chill this dressing to let the flavors meld.

"No one is you, and that is your [superpower.]" —Dave Grohl

VARIATION
For an amazing dip, thicken the dressing by blending it with ½ avocado.

lemon caesar dressing

Oh boy, is this delicious! There's a bit of technique to preparing this dressing, because you have to add the olive oil very gradually to ensure that it emulsifies with your mayonnaise, but once you master it, you'll feel like a rock star. It's good with any salad, steak, chicken, or as a dipping sauce. MAKES 1 CUP • COOK TIME: 10 MINUTES

Put the egg in a large mason jar. While blending with an immersion blender, slowly add the olive oil in a thin stream and blend until emulsified.

Add the preserved lemon, anchovies, and garlic to the jar and blend until smooth. Add the lemon juice, mustard, and pepper and blend until combined well. If the dressing seems too thick, blend in 1 to 2 tablespoons water. Taste and season with salt, stirring to combine.

Use immediately or store in an airtight container in the refrigerator for up to 6 days.

1 large egg

¾ cup light extra-virgin olive oil

2 tablespoons chopped Preserved Meyer Lemon (page 38), pressed through a garlic press

2 anchovy fillets

2 garlic cloves, pressed

2 tablespoons fresh lemon juice

½ teaspoon Dijon mustard (check label for compliance if doing Whole30)

½ teaspoon freshly ground black pepper

Kosher salt

PAIRS WITH . . .

Steak Lemon Caesar (page 117); great with Everyday Greens (page 282), Green Beans Almondine (page 266), Chicken Sausage and Fingerling Potatoes (page 151), or with fish or a simple kale salad.

TERI'S TIPS

Toss this dressing with chopped roasted chicken breast (see page 143) and chopped Marinated Red Onions (page 30) for an insanely delicious chicken salad.

creamy horseradish dressing

GLUTEN-FREE
DAIRY-FREE
WHOLE30
PALEO
GRAIN-FREE

This classic dressing combines the sharpness of horseradish with the creaminess of Whole30-compliant mayo for a sublime treat. Find fresh horseradish root, because the flavor is absolutely worth the moment of effort. MAKES 1¼ CUPS • COOK TIME: 15 MINUTES

1 cup Whole30 Mayonnaise (page 286)

¼ to ½ cup grated fresh horse-radish

1 teaspoon Dijon mustard (check label for compliance if doing Whole30)

1 tablespoon red wine vinegar

½ teaspoon kosher salt

¼ teaspoon freshly ground black pepper

2 tablespoons finely chopped fresh chives

In a food processor, combine the mayonnaise, ¼ cup of the horseradish, the mustard, vinegar, salt, and pepper. Process until the dressing is smooth and creamy. Taste and add up to ¼ cup of the remaining horseradish, as desired.

Transfer to a bowl, add the chives, and stir to combine. Serve immediately or store in an airtight container in the refrigerator for up to 5 days.

PAIRS WITH . . .

BLT Salad (page 124), Slow-Roasted Beef Eye of Round (page 184), Asian Steak Salad (page 115), Tomato Salad (page 126), a hard-boiled egg and Marinated Red Onions (page 30); great on fish, with potatoes, or as a dressing for coleslaw or as a dipping sauce for Patrick's Chicken Fingers (page 251) or Cassava-Crusted Calamari (page 222).

TERI'S TIPS

All horseradish is different, so start with ¼ cup and add more as needed, up to ½ cup.

---

grapefruit-lime vinaigrette

I love a special sauce that elevates food from ordinary to extraordinary, and this one does it with ease. Think vinaigrette, but so much more. It's fresh, updated, and Whole30. It's a home run! MAKES ABOUT ½ CUP • COOK TIME: 10 MINUTES

In small bowl, whisk together the grapefruit and lime juices, then, while whisking, slowly add the oil in a thin stream and whisk until emulsified. Stir in the garlic confit, serrano, basil, salt, and black pepper. Taste for sweetness, and if the grapefruit isn't sweet enough, add the orange juice. Season with more salt and the pepper, if needed.

Use immediately or store in an airtight container in the refrigerator for up to 5 days.

PAIRS WITH . . .
Chicken Finger Salad (page 109) and Roy's Chicken and Cheddar Potato Stack (page 149); toss with greens; use as a lovely sauce for Citrus Cod (page 203); thicken it up with some mango to create a tropical-inspired sauce; mix with ¼ cup Whole30 Mayonnaise (page 286) to make a delicious sauce.

¼ cup fresh grapefruit juice (from ½ medium Ruby Red grapefruit)

1 tablespoon fresh lime juice

¼ cup extra-virgin olive oil

1 clove Garlic Confit (page 33), pressed

1 tablespoon minced fresh serrano pepper

1 teaspoon finely chopped fresh basil leaves

½ teaspoon kosher salt, plus more if needed

⅛ teaspoon freshly ground black pepper, plus more if needed

1 tablespoon fresh orange juice (optional)

"Everyone needs someone who will call and say: Get dressed, we're going on an adventure."
—Unknown

zesty garlic-tahini dressing

GLUTEN-FREE
DAIRY-FREE
WHOLE30
PALEO
GRAIN-FREE

Run, don't walk, to make this! The combination of zest, tang, garlic, and lemon adds quite a delicious bite. If you haven't discovered tahini as a Whole30 cooking ingredient, it is lusciously compliant. My local Middle Eastern store is a wonderful source for so many ingredients, and they make the best tahini—it's worth making a special trip to a store that makes it fresh. **MAKES ABOUT 1 CUP • COOK TIME: 10 MINUTES**

¼ cup plus 2 tablespoons tahini (sesame paste)

¼ cup fresh lemon juice

3 tablespoons extra-virgin olive oil

1 tablespoon plus 1½ teaspoons red wine vinegar

5 garlic cloves

¾ teaspoon kosher salt, plus more if needed

⅓ cup chopped fresh cilantro

2 scallions, sliced

In a medium bowl, mix ¼ cup water, the tahini, lemon juice, olive oil, and vinegar until combined well. Set aside.

On a cutting board, use the side of a chef's knife to mash the garlic cloves. When they start to become juicy, add the salt and mash it with the garlic until combined and broken down into a paste.

Add the mashed garlic to the bowl with the tahini mixture and stir until combined well. Transfer to a food processor, add the cilantro and scallions, and process until smooth. Taste and add more salt, if needed. If the dressing seems too thick, add a bit more water.

Use immediately or store in an airtight container in the refrigerator for up to 5 days.

"And suddenly. You know . . . It's time to start something new and trust the magic of beginnings."
—Meister Eckhart

PAIRS WITH . . .
Jerusalem Salad (page 131), Chicken Shawarma (page 111), kale (in a salad or sautéed); delicious tossed with French green beans or cauliflower fried rice, or in a lettuce wrap sandwich; makes a great dipping sauce for roasted chicken breast, skirt steak, lamb, or fish.

creamy leek slaw

Sometimes the best dishes are truly simple. This leek slaw is great served with fish, paired with pork, or even slathered on a hamburger. Leeks have a flavor that's like a very herbaceous onion, and they bring a satisfying crunch and bold taste to this slaw—that can double as a sauce. MAKES ABOUT 2 CUPS • COOK TIME: 5 MINUTES

In a medium bowl, mix the leeks, mayonnaise, salt, and pepper until combined well.

Use immediately or store in an airtight container in the refrigerator for up to 3 days.

2 large leeks, white and pale green parts only, halved lengthwise and sliced into ⅛-inch-thick half-moons (about 2 cups)

1 cup Whole30 Mayonnaise (page 286)

½ teaspoon kosher salt

¼ teaspoon freshly ground black pepper

> ### TERI'S TIPS
> To wash leeks properly, with the root attached, split them in half length-wise and fan them a bit under cool running water to rinse away any dirt that might be between the layers. Trim away the root end and slice the tender stalks into half-moons.
>
> ### PAIRS WITH . . .
> Bone-In Pork Schnitzel (page 171), Skillet-Seared Sirloin (page 181), and Not Your Mother's Meat Loaf (page 252); blend in ¼ cup Tomato Confit (page 35) to create a delicious sauce.

golden onion sauce

So simple, yet a bit of a masterpiece, this recipe very naturally creates a Whole30 gravy that's delicious with pork, beef, and anything else that calls for a simple gravy. It's hard to find a Whole30-compliant one, but this is it, folks. Patience is a virtue. While I'd really like to give you the exact cooking time, caramelizing depends on the onion, the pan, the stove—and even when I make it, it's different every time. Watch for the onions to be a rich honey or wheat color and caramelized on the edges. Once you get your own timing down, be sure to make a note here in the book, so you'll know how long it may take you next time. **MAKES ¾ TO 1 CUP • COOK TIME: 30 MINUTES**

2   tablespoons clarified butter

2   cups thinly sliced yellow onions

½   teaspoon kosher salt

1   cup Chicken Stock (page 47), warmed

1   teaspoon pressed Garlic Confit (page 33)

⅛   teaspoon ground white pepper

PAIRS WITH . . .
Bone-In Pork Schnitzel (page 171), mashed potatoes, cauliflower rice, or vegetables.

In large sauté pan, melt the clarified butter over medium heat. Add the onions and salt and cook, stirring continuously, until the onions are light golden brown, 7 to 9 minutes. Reduce the heat to medium-low and remove any burnt onion. Cook, stirring continuously, until caramelized, 12 to 15 minutes more. Remove the pan from the heat.

In a food processor, combine ½ cup of the stock, the caramelized onions, garlic confit, and white pepper and blend until smooth. Add the remaining stock a bit at a time, until the desired consistency is reached (you may not use it all).

Serve immediately or store in an airtight container in the refrigerator for up to 5 days.

smoky red pepper sauce

Simple. Legendary. Don't underestimate the magic of charring peppers and blending them with red wine vinegar. The balance of the smoky with the tang and the creamy is perfect for a sauce, a salad dressing, or a dip. Some people I know even enjoy it by the spoonful. MAKES 2 CUPS • COOK TIME: 35 MINUTES

Preheat the broiler and raise the oven rack to 5 or 6 inches below the heat source.

Put the bell peppers on a baking sheet and drizzle evenly with the olive oil. Sprinkle ½ teaspoon of the salt and the black pepper over them. Broil until charred, about 15 minutes. Flip the peppers over and broil, flipping every 5 minutes until completely charred, 10 to 15 minutes more. Remove the peppers from the oven and let cool.

Remove and discard the charred skin, seeds, and stems and transfer the flesh from the peppers to a blender or food processor. Add the mayonnaise, vinegar, the remaining 1 teaspoon salt, the hot sauce, and the cayenne and blend until smooth.

Serve immediately or store in an airtight container in the refrigerator for up to 3 days.

2 medium red bell peppers (see Tip)
1 teaspoon extra-virgin olive oil
1½ teaspoons kosher salt
¼ teaspoon freshly ground black pepper
1 cup Whole30 Mayonnaise (page 286)
2 tablespoons red wine vinegar
1 teaspoon hot sauce (check label for compliance if doing Whole30)
¼ teaspoon cayenne pepper

PAIRS WITH . . .
Tangy Stuffed Baked Potatoes (page 279), Gluten-Free Summer Corn and Zucchini Fritters (page 276), and Fajita Steak Platter (page 176); also great served with taco lettuce wraps, or any Mexican- or Spanish-inspired dishes.

TERI'S TIPS
To make peeling really easy, broil the peppers a day ahead. When the peppers are out of the oven, put them in a paper bag for about an hour, then peel; the skins will come right off.

"Those who don't believe in magic will never find it."
—Roald Dahl

spicy almond sauce

This delicious and easy alternative to a peanut sauce is light, spicy, and wonderful. You don't need to talk people into this, and it works as a dipping sauce, a dressing, or a creamy complement to a stir-fry.

SERVES 4 • COOK TIME: 10 MINUTES

1 cup full-fat unsweetened coconut milk, blended

¼ cup plus 1 tablespoon almond butter

¼ cup chopped scallions

3 tablespoons coconut aminos

2 tablespoons rice wine vinegar

1 tablespoon hot sauce (check label for compliance if you're doing Whole30)

1 tablespoon dark toasted sesame oil

1 red Fresno pepper, seeded and chopped

2 garlic cloves, pressed

Juice from 1 tablespoon grated fresh ginger (see page 296)

¼ to ½ teaspoon cayenne pepper (depending on your spice preference)

In a food processor or blender, combine the coconut milk and almond butter and blend until smooth. Add the scallions, coconut aminos, vinegar, hot sauce, sesame oil, Fresno pepper, garlic, ginger juice, and cayenne and blend until smooth.

Use immediately or store in an airtight container in the refrigerator for up to 4 days.

PAIRS WITH . . .

Shrimp Pad Thai (page 119), Asian Steak Salad (page 115), and Grandma Post's Egg Rolls (page 256); great served with beef satay; use it as a dressing to create an Asian-style slaw.

cashew crema

GLUTEN-FREE

DAIRY-FREE

WHOLE30

PALEO

GRAIN-FREE

This rich and velvety topping is a fantastic addition to so many dishes. Add a dollop of this concoction to a roasted chicken breast or zucchini roll-up, use it as a topper on an hors d'oeuvre, or incorporate it into a spicy sauce to serve with grilled pork chops. It's super easy to make, and it's vegan! MAKES 1 CUP •

COOK TIME: 6 MINUTES, PLUS UP TO 2 HOURS SOAKING TIME (SEE TIP)

1   cup raw cashews

¼ to ½   teaspoon kosher salt

VARIATION
Blend in 1 teaspoon finely fresh chopped chives (my favorite), ½ teaspoon dried thyme, or 3 or 4 fresh basil leaves.

Put the cashews in a medium bowl and pour over enough water to cover the cashews by 1 inch. Soak for at least 2 hours or as long as overnight. Drain and rinse well.

In a food processor, combine the cashews, ¼ teaspoon of the salt, and ¼ cup cold water and process until smooth, 2 minutes. Using a rubber spatula, scrape down the sides. Add another ¼ cup water and process until creamy and smooth, 3 to 4 minutes more. If you prefer a thinner consistency, adjust the water accordingly. Taste and add the remaining salt as needed.

Use immediately or store in an airtight container in the refrigerator for up to 4 days.

PAIRS WITH . . .
Patrick's Vegetarian Feast (page 269) and Sweet Potato Crostini Topped with Mushrooms (page 273); great blended with Tomato Confit (page 35) or Garlic Confit (page 33) to make a delicious sauce.

TERI'S TIPS
If you don't have the time to soak the cashews for 2 hours, you can put the cashews and 2 cups water in a pot and bring to a boil. Boil for 15 minutes, then drain and rinse well and proceed as directed.

breakfast

My equation for an everyday Whole30 breakfast is simple:

Leftovers + Greens + Marinated Red Onions + an Optional Egg = Exceptional Breakfast

My favorite Whole30 breakfasts are repurposed leftovers from the previous night, and my favorite dinners have elements that can become my next day's breakfast. If that appeals to you, too, you'll be thrilled to hear that this book is full of dinner ideas that lend themselves to an excellent breakfast. These recipes are for those weekend mornings when you have a bit more time on your hands, or when you want to create something special for guests. I happen to enjoy greens for breakfast, and I love knowing I've gotten my greens in first thing. It's a great way to start the day, and it's a two-fer, because greens are a fantastic bed for your leftovers.

chilaquiles

Speaking as a gal who loves chilaquiles, I'm crazy about my grain-free Whole30 version. Although this dish takes bit of prep, the sweet potato crisps can be done a couple of hours ahead. My Tomato Confit mixed with spices and canned tomatoes is a fabulous recipe hack that will leave you with a sauce that is something wonderful. I top the chilaquiles with a fried or scrambled egg. I now prefer this recipe over the classic tortilla version. Warning: You might have to hide the sweet potato crisps in the process—not just from other people, but from yourself! SERVES 4 • COOK TIME: 40 MINUTES

Preheat the oven to 350°F.

In a saucepan, combine the crushed tomatoes with their juices, garlic, smoked paprika, cayenne, coriander, and salt and cook over medium heat, stirring, until warm, about 2 minutes. Transfer to a blender, add the tomato confit and oil, and blend for 25 seconds, until smooth. Return the sauce to the pan; set aside.

Meanwhile, in a large cast-iron pan, heat the olive oil over medium heat. Add the sausages and cook, stirring, until heated through and browned, 6 to 7 minutes. Transfer the sausages to a plate and set aside.

In a large bowl, combine the sweet potato crisps and ⅓ cup of the sauce and toss to coat the crisps thoroughly and evenly. Transfer the contents of the bowl to the cast-iron pan you used for the sausages and bake for 8 minutes, or until warmed through.

Meanwhile, cook the eggs to your liking.

Remove the pan from the oven and top the chilaquiles with the eggs and the sausages (reheat them, if needed).

Serve the chilaquiles directly from the pan. Reheat the remaining sauce, if needed, and serve it on the side.

Sweet Potato Crisps (page 288)

3 cups canned crushed tomatoes, undrained

2 teaspoons pressed garlic

2 teaspoons smoked paprika

1 teaspoon cayenne pepper

¼ teaspoon ground coriander

½ teaspoon kosher salt

½ cup Tomato Confit (page 35) with some of the oil

1 tablespoon extra-virgin olive oil

12 ounces Whole30-compliant pre-cooked smoked chorizo sausages, sliced into ¼-inch-thick rounds

4 large eggs

TERI'S TIPS

The crisps can be done a couple of hours in advance, but don't combine them with the sauce until you're ready to serve them.

spring breakfast

While typically I love a crispy potato, here I've kept it simple by combining parboiled, tender fingerling potatoes with spring asparagus. Finished off with the richness of an egg, this dish is great for a weekend breakfast or brunch, but you might want it every day of the week. Enough said. Try this served with Tomato Confit (page 35) or Pistachio Pesto (page 51). SERVES 4 • COOK TIME: 25 MINUTES

1 tablespoon plus
  1½ teaspoons kosher salt

1 pound fingerling potatoes

1 pound asparagus

2 tablespoons clarified butter

¼ cup sliced shallots

½ teaspoon freshly ground
  black pepper

4 large eggs, poached
  (see Tip)

TERI'S TIPS

To poach eggs, fill a large sauté pan three-quarters full with water and bring the water to a boil over high heat. Crack each egg into an individual small bowl and, one at a time, gently slide the eggs into the boiling water. Gently slide a slotted spoon under the egg so the egg doesn't stick to the bottom of the pan. Cook for 2½ to 3 minutes, then remove with a slotted spoon.

In a medium pot, bring 2 quarts water and 1 tablespoon of the salt to a boil over high heat. Add the potatoes. Cover and cook until they're just cooked through, about 10 minutes. Drain the potatoes and let cool. Cut the potatoes in half lengthwise and set aside.

Cut the woody ends off the asparagus, peel the rough layer off the ends of the stalks, and cut the stalks into thirds. Set aside.

In a large sauté pan, melt the clarified butter over medium heat, tilting the pan to coat the bottom. Arrange the potatoes cut-side down in the pan, sprinkle with ¾ teaspoon of the salt, and cook for 2 minutes. Add the shallots, asparagus, remaining ¾ teaspoon salt, and the pepper and cook for 2 minutes more. Gently toss the vegetables together, cover, and cook for 2 minutes more. Uncover, toss again, cover, and cook for 2 minutes more. Repeat until vegetables are tender, 4 to 6 minutes more.

Serve on a large platter or individual plates, with the poached eggs on top.

"I don't think any day is worth living without thinking about what you're going to eat next at all times." —Nora Ephron

zucchini pie

This is a summertime treat, perfect for zucchini season. Layers of thinly sliced zucchini, shallots, and egg are infused with Tomato Confit and finished off with crispy bacon and ribbons of fresh basil. Vary this dish by using seasonal vegetables, different spice profiles, red bell pepper, or even precooked sausage. If you're not doing Whole30, crumbles of mozzarella or feta take it up a notch. Once you have mastered this frittata, make it a hundred different ways. SERVES 4 • COOK TIME: 1 HOUR

In a large bowl, toss the zucchini with 1 teaspoon of the salt. Spread out a tea towel and arrange the zucchini slices on the towel in a single layer. Cover the zucchini with another tea towel, press down lightly, and let sit for 20 minutes to draw out excess moisture.

Preheat the oven to 350°F.

In a blender or food processor, combine the eggs, coconut milk, remaining ¼ teaspoon salt and ⅛ teaspoon of the pepper and blend until thoroughly combined. Set aside.

In a cast-iron pan, heat 2 teaspoons of the olive oil over medium heat. Add the shallots and cook, stirring, until soft and light brown, about 2 minutes. Transfer the shallots to a plate and set aside.

In the same pan, heat the remaining 2 tablespoons oil over medium heat. Add the zucchini slices and cook, stirring occasionally, until translucent, 8 to 10 minutes.

Stir in the garlic and the shallots and turn off the heat. Evenly distribute the tomato confit over the top and press down lightly to evenly flatten the ingredients. Sprinkle with the remaining ⅛ teaspoon pepper and pour the egg mixture into the pan. Bake for 12 to 15 minutes, until cooked through and springy to the touch in the middle. Remove from the oven and let stand for 5 minutes before slicing into wedges. Top with bacon and basil and serve.

6	cups thinly sliced zucchini
1¼	teaspoons kosher salt
8	large eggs
¼	cup full-fat canned coconut milk, blended
¼	teaspoon freshly ground black pepper
2	tablespoons plus 2 teaspoons extra-virgin olive oil
½	cup sliced shallots
4	cloves Garlic Confit (page 33), pressed
1	scant cup drained Tomato Confit (page 35)
	Perfect Oven Bacon (page 294), sliced into 1-inch pieces, for topping
2	tablespoons chopped fresh basil leaves

TERI'S TIPS

Zucchini is a vegetable full of water, so you want to be sure to sweat out the water thoroughly. Even if your zucchini is extra wet, don't worry—cut it up, sweat it out, and use it.

gluten-free chocolate chip buttermilk oatcakes

There's no greater joy than waking my kids with the smell of pancakes on the weekend. Everyone's a little gentler in the morning, and it's a special time when sweet memories are made. It reminds me of slumber parties. Adapted from my sister P.S.'s kitchen. SERVES 6 TO 8; MAKES 20 PANCAKES • COOK TIME: 1¼ HOURS

In a large bowl, combine the oats and buttermilk and let sit for 20 minutes.

Add the eggs and butter and stir well. Add the oat flour, sugar, baking powder, baking soda, and salt and stir gently. Gently stir in the chocolate chips. Let stand for 10 minutes.

In a large nonstick stainless steel pan, melt 1 tablespoon of the coconut oil over medium heat. Using a ¼-cup measure, add the batter to the pan, leaving room between pancakes for flipping. Cook until bubbles appear throughout the center and the pancakes are cooked around the edges and golden brown on the bottom, 3 to 4 minutes, then carefully flip. Note that this is a very delicate batter, so don't flip too soon or they will fall apart. Cook for 2 to 3 minutes on the second side, until the pancakes are cooked through, watching them so that they do not burn. Remove and set aside. Repeat to cook the remaining batter.

Serve sprinkled with pecans and drizzled with maple syrup.

2	cups old-fashioned rolled oats
2½	cups buttermilk
2	large eggs, beaten
4	tablespoons (½ stick) unsalted butter, melted and cooled
¾	cup plus 2 tablespoons oat flour
2	tablespoons coconut sugar
1	teaspoon baking powder
1	teaspoon baking soda
¼	teaspoon kosher salt
½	cup gluten-free chocolate chips
5	tablespoons coconut oil or oil of your choice
½	cup chopped pecans
	Maple syrup, for serving

"Be happy in the moment, that's enough. Each moment is all we need, not more." —Mother Teresa

TERI'S TIPS

To make your own oat flour, grind rolled oats in the food processor for two minutes, then stir it, measure, and add. Or try using gluten-free flour—but not all gluten-free flours are equal, so be prepared to play with the amount of flour to achieve the best consistency.

TERI'S TIPS

Nature can provide you with a perfect tool. Whenever I'm making eggs, I find the ideal measurement to make them creamy is a half eggshell of water per egg.

If you are taking it to-go for lunch, be sure to add my Marinated Red Onions.

If you don't have leftover chicken to use and need to quickly make some cutlets, here's what you do: Sprinkle a pinch of kosher salt, freshly ground black pepper, hot paprika, and granulated garlic evenly over each chicken cutlet. In a sauté pan, heat a bit of olive oil over medium-high heat. Cook the cutlets for 3 minutes per side.

broccolini and chicken breakfast hash with softly scrambled eggs

My friend Michael from Symmetry Breakfast once told me, "When cooking or prepping ahead, make sure you pull aside tomorrow's lunch or leftovers first." Truer words were never spoken. As a person who tends to overdo it a bit, it's a great idea for portion control. I think one of the tricks to a successful Whole30 is thinking smart by doing a little extra at dinner and repurposing it for future meals. Often, I double an entire recipe, so I can use it the next day, or I just make a couple of extra chicken breasts while I'm cooking. This very quick breakfast hash is a play on both doubling a recipe and repurposing a dish in a way that makes it fresh, new, and delicious. SERVES 2 • COOK TIME: 15 MINUTES

2 tablespoons extra-virgin olive oil

3 cups roughly sliced Broccolini (about 1 bunch)

2 cloves Garlic Confit (page 33), chopped (optional)

½ teaspoon kosher salt

1 leftover cooked boneless, skinless chicken breast, cut into ½-inch cubes (see Tip)

4 large eggs

1 avocado, sliced (optional)

Marinated Red Onions (page 30; optional)

Gomasio (page 36; optional)

In a large sauté pan, heat 1 tablespoon of the olive oil over medium-high heat. Add the Broccolini and cook, stirring, until crisp-tender, about 3 minutes. Add the garlic confit, salt, and chicken. Cook, stirring, until thoroughly heated through, about 2 minutes, then set aside on a plate.

Using a whisk or a blender, beat the eggs in a bowl until frothy. Then add 4 half eggshells of water (about 6 tablespoons) and beat until combined well. Set the mixture aside.

In the same pan you used for the Broccolini, heat the remaining 1 tablespoon oil over low heat. Pour the beaten eggs into the pan and gently cook, stirring continuously, until softly scrambled, about 5 minutes.

Spoon the hash onto a plate and top it with the scrambled eggs. Serve with avocado, marinated red onions, and gomasio, if desired.

gluten-free blueberry crumble

GLUTEN-FREE

I'm so excited to share this amazing family favorite. As a gluten-free person, I have found it takes a bit of sorcery to produce a dish that everybody loves, gluten-free or not. It could almost be a Magic Elixir, it's just that fabulous! The trick is to leave the crust soft and chewy, because the natural syrup from the blueberries combined with the sumptuous crust make it perfect for breakfast. It's also fantastic for dessert. You're welcome. SERVES 6 TO 8 • COOK TIME: 45 MINUTES

Preheat the oven to 350°F. Thoroughly grease a 9 × 11- or 8 × 11-inch baking dish with 2 teaspoons of the butter.

In a small, dry skillet, cook the pecans over low heat, stirring occasionally, until fragrant and lightly toasted, about 8 minutes. Remove from the pan, coarsely chop, and set aside.

In a small saucepan, melt the remaining ½ cup (1 stick) butter over low heat. Remove the pan from the heat and set aside.

In a medium bowl, mix together the blueberries, granulated sugar, lemon zest, and cornstarch. Add the lemon juice, stirring gently to combine well. Pour the mixture into the prepared baking dish and set aside.

In a medium bowl, stir together the rolled oats, brown sugar, oat flour, and salt. Add the pecans and stir. Pour in the melted butter and stir to combine. Spoon the mixture evenly over the blueberries.

Bake until bubbling, 25 to 30 minutes (see Tip). Remove from the oven and let cool for 10 minutes.

It's delicious warm or at room temperature. Do not refrigerate.

"A party without a cake is just a meeting." —Julia Child

½ cup (1 stick) plus 2 teaspoons unsalted butter

½ cup pecans

4 cups fresh blueberries

¼ cup plus 2 tablespoons granulated sugar, plus more if needed

2 tablespoons grated lemon zest

2 tablespoons cornstarch

1 tablespoon fresh lemon juice

1 cup old-fashioned rolled oats

¾ cup brown sugar, packed

½ cup oat flour

½ teaspoon kosher salt

TERI'S TIPS
The cooking time for this recipe is always a debate in my family. I like a soft, chewy crust, and this is perfect for me at 20 minutes. Others like it crunchy and cook it for up to 26 minutes.

soups and sandwiches

There is an ancient alchemy that happens when a group of well-chosen ingredients is bound together with love—it is a Magic Elixir for healing. A luscious bowl of soup is like a bowl of soul. Spend an afternoon making one of these favorites with your family, and you will see what I mean: you can taste the love.

While in Michigan with Roy for a weekend, I saw a sign that said, "Life is like a sandwich: you have to fill it with the best ingredients." All I can say to that is YES. While remodeling my basement, I made the contractors sandwiches daily, and not only were my followers riveted when I posted the stories, but I'm quite sure the construction took weeks longer because of those sandwiches. My dedication to finding the most delicious sandwich ingredients is matched by my enthusiasm about making a special sauce. For a legendary sandwich, the ingredients absolutely have to be curated. Whether it's ham, bread, cheese, or greens, I love the concept of a sandwich as a masterpiece.

quick rotisserie chicken soup

Chicken soup is such a soul-satisfying dish, and here's a genius hack: start with a grocery store rotisserie or baked chicken, pull it off the bone, and use the carcass to make a last-minute stock for a weeknight dinner that is super-infused with flavor. It comes together quickly, but tastes like you fussed all day. This is delicious served with Sweet Potato Crisps (page 288). **SERVES 4 • COOK TIME: 35 MINUTES**

Pull the chicken meat off the bone, reserving the bones and skin, then separate the meat into two groups: 1) the best of the meat to add at the end to the finished soup, and 2) the less-enticing, not-so-pretty pieces to cook in the broth with the bones and skin. Pull the nicer-looking, soup-worthy chicken meat apart into pieces about the size of your pinky finger and set aside.

In a large pot, heat the olive oil over medium-high heat. Add the reserved (not-so-pretty) chicken meat, skin, and bones and cook, stirring, for 3 minutes. Add ½ teaspoon of the salt and 5 cups water and stir to combine. Add the halved carrot, the celery, and the garlic and bring to a boil. Turn the heat to low and gently simmer for 15 minutes. Strain the broth and discard the solids.

In a small sauté pan, melt the clarified butter over medium-high heat. Add the sliced carrot and ¼ teaspoon of the salt and cook, stirring, until just tender, 3 to 4 minutes. Set aside.

Bring a medium pot of water to a boil with 2 teaspoons of the salt. Prepare a large bowl of ice water. Blanch the green beans in the boiling water for 5 minutes. Drain the beans and immediately plunge them into the bowl of ice water. Drain again; set aside.

Warm the broth over medium heat. Add the shredded chicken, green beans, and carrots (with any pan juices). Season with the remaining ½ teaspoon salt and the pepper. Stir in the rotisserie juices. When ready to serve, garnish with the parsley.

1	whole rotisserie chicken, juices from the container reserved
1	tablespoon extra-virgin olive oil
3¼	teaspoons kosher salt
2	large carrots: 1 halved lengthwise, 1 sliced into coins
1	medium celery stalk, halved lengthwise
1	garlic clove, pressed
1	tablespoon clarified butter
1½	cups green beans, halved
½	teaspoon freshly ground black pepper
¼	cup chopped fresh parsley, for garnish

TERI'S TIPS
Double this recipe to have leftovers.

"Only the pure at heart can make a good soup."
—Ludwig van Beethoven

TERI'S TIPS

Chorizo comes in many different ways. If you get the precooked version, follow my directions. If it isn't precooked, cook it per the directions on the package.

Two examples of Whole30- compliant brands are Wellshire Farms and Pederson's Natural Farms.

portuguese stew

There's nothing like a seafood stew. It's a classic, and always a favorite for me. This updated version is so special. The chicken stock–infused clams, sausage, broken-up potatoes, and tomato confit create a magnificent combination of spicy, rich, and delicious. Perfect for company and an ultimate one-dish meal. It's ideal served with a simple arugula salad. SERVES 4 • COOK TIME: 45 MINUTES

2 tablespoons clarified butter

1 large white onion, chopped

3 garlic cloves, chopped

24 ounces precooked pork chorizo (check label for compliance if doing Whole30), sliced into ¼-inch-thick rounds

1 tablespoon red wine vinegar

1 teaspoon red pepper flakes

6 cups Chicken Stock (page 47)

1½ pound fingerling or red potatoes, quartered

1 cup cut green beans (½-inch pieces)

1 large carrot, cut into ¼-inch slices

3 pounds clams, such as littleneck

¼ cup Tomato Confit, chopped (page 35)

¼ cup crushed canned tomatoes, undrained

"We must be willing to let go of the life we planned so as to have the life that is waiting for us."
—Joseph Campbell

In a Dutch oven, melt the clarified butter over medium-high heat. Add the onion and cook, stirring, until translucent and soft, about 2 minutes. Add the garlic and cook, stirring, until fragrant, about 1 minute. Add the chorizo, stir to combine, and cook until the chorizo is browned, about 5 minutes. Add the vinegar and the red pepper flakes and stir to combine well. Turn off the heat and set aside.

In a separate pot, bring the stock to a boil over medium-high heat. Add the potatoes, stir while the stock comes back to a boil, then cook for 3 minutes. Add the green beans and boil for 4 minutes more. Add the carrots and cook until the carrots are just tender and the potatoes are cooked through, 1 to 2 minutes. Using a slotted spoon, transfer the vegetables from the stock to the Dutch oven.

Add the clams to the stock and return the stock to a boil. Cook until the clams begin to open, usually after about 3 minutes. Spoon the clams into the Dutch oven, discarding any that have not opened, and add all but about 1 cup of the stock from the pot. Stir the tomato confit into the reserved 1 cup stock and cook for 1 minute. Add the crushed tomatoes and stir to combine. Pour the tomato mixture into the Dutch oven and stir.

Bring the Dutch oven to the table and let everyone serve themselves.

shrimp coconut bowl

GLUTEN-FREE
WHOLE30
PALEO
GRAIN-FREE

This is less of a soup and more of an "in-the-shell shrimp in a little bit of broth" dish. It's truly divine! My tip here is to cook the shrimp with the shells on, though most people are used to cooking them without. I'm here to tell you that leaving them on is the secret ingredient to making this dish great—and there's no need to worry, you can devein the shrimp with the shells intact. Served in just a bit of coconut broth, this dish should be eaten with close friends or true foodies. Don't try to be polite: reach your hands into the serving bowl, grab the succulent shrimp, peel, and devour. SERVES 4 • COOK TIME: 1 HOUR

1¼ pounds large shell-on shrimp, deveined (see Tip)

2 tablespoons grated fresh ginger

3 tablespoons grated fresh turmeric

2 tablespoons clarified butter

2 cups sliced Broccolini (stems sliced, florets kept whole)

1 cup chopped green beans (1-inch pieces)

1½ teaspoons kosher salt

¾ teaspoon freshly ground black pepper

2 tablespoons coconut oil

¼ cup thinly sliced shallots

1 garlic clove, thinly sliced

½ cup thinly sliced scallions

2 tablespoons finely chopped lemongrass

2 cups Chicken Stock (page 47), warmed

Put the shrimp in a large bowl and squeeze the juice from the ginger and the juice from 2 tablespoons of the grated turmeric over the shrimp. Toss well, then cover with plastic wrap and refrigerate for 10 minutes.

In a medium pot, melt the clarified butter over medium heat. Add the Broccolini, green beans, ½ teaspoon of the salt, and ¼ teaspoon of the black pepper, stir to combine, and cook until the vegetables turn bright green and tender but are still crisp, about 3 minutes. Remove the beans and Broccolini from the pot and set aside.

In the same pot, melt the coconut oil over medium heat. Add the shallots and garlic and cook, stirring, until fragrant but not browned, about 30 seconds. Add the scallions, lemongrass, and ½ teaspoon of the salt and cook until softened, about 1 minute more. Add 2 cups of the stock and stir well, scraping up all the caramelized bits from the bottom of the pan. Add the lime leaves and chile, stir, and bring to a simmer. Cook for 2 to 3 minutes.

continued...

Stir in the coconut milk, then add the shrimp, remaining ½ teaspoon salt, remaining ½ teaspoon black pepper, and the cayenne and stir to combine well. Bring back to a simmer and cook until the shrimp are just cooked through, about 3 minutes.

In a small bowl, combine the coconut aminos, lime juice, and the juice from the remaining 1 tablespoon grated turmeric. Mix well, then add to the pot. Add the sautéed vegetables and the spinach to the pot and cook, stirring gently, for 1 minute more.

Serve garnished with cilantro, with lime wedges alongside.

"Cooking is like love: It should be entered into with abandon or not at all."
—Harriet Van Horne

2	Kaffir lime leaves (optional)
1	red Thai chile or other spicy fresh red chile, seeded and sliced, or 1 dried Thai chile
1	cup full-fat unsweetened coconut milk, blended
¼	teaspoon cayenne pepper
2	tablespoons coconut aminos
1	tablespoon fresh lime juice
1	cup spinach leaves
	Fresh cilantro leaves, for garnish
	Lime wedges, for garnish

TERI'S TIPS

Cooking shrimp with the shell on is simply more delicious. It's possible to devein the shrimp and keep the shell on: Insert the tip of your kitchen shears just under the shell on the shrimp's back, where the head was, and gently cut through the shell (not the shrimp meat) down to the base of the tail, then remove the vein with your fingers, leaving the tail intact.

Save the shrimp shells, which can make an amazing stock.

If you prefer more of a soup, just double the stock.

You can find the Kaffir lime leaves in many Asian grocery stores; they freeze well.

making a difference

I've been extended so much grace in my life, beginning with having amazing parents who truly believed in me and my sisters. We grew up knowing that a lot is expected from those who have been given a lot. My parents were fortunate people, and they lived by that conviction. They would give quietly, which meant that I would sometimes find out years later that they had paid for someone's education. When I was a little girl, I discovered my mom had donated a piano to the church anonymously. I asked her why it had been anonymous, and she said, "Don't give a piano to the church if you have to tell people about it."

Through my parents, I learned that each of us should do whatever we can within our sphere of influence, to whatever extent possible. Certainly, the greatest heartbreak of my lifetime was losing my parents. The gift that they left me with is this: a clear sense of how I decide to make a difference. I am eternally grateful for who they were and how they live on through me.

My mom was the original "unconditional acts of kindness" woman. My sisters and I followed her around with glee and delight as she did things like pay the toll for the car behind us and then zoom off, so they wouldn't know who it was. She simply enjoyed bringing a moment of joy into others' lives. Any time you can have a positive impact on someone else, don't think about it—just do it.

The best way to honor my parents' memory and thank them is to live the best life I can. Part of that for me is paying it forward. The day my dad died, I held his hand and said, "You've had a great life." And he looked at me with joyful tears streaming down his face and said, "I really have. I really have. I think I made a difference." Here was a man who had a truly amazing life, but in his last moments, this was what mattered to him most. Though my parents died years ago, they remain a major influence in my life.

There is a saying, "From generation to generation." That is how I try to honor my parents, by making a difference. I believe that

my children will do the same. In my own small way, I am trying to leave the world a better place than I found it.

Life is a wonderful adventure and can be a heck of a lot more fun when we are looking for our own unique way to make a difference. Here's an idea: unconditional acts of kindness, speaking out for what we know is wrong, being in service to a friend in need—even if it's just opening a door or sharing your Marinated Red Onions with them—will help build stronger communities and happier neighborhoods. Make a good day better by smiling at someone. It can be that simple.

salami gruyère sinky
sandwich with pepperoncini mayonnaise

Crunchy, bubbly, salty, briny, and spicy, this sandwich demands a cloth napkin. In fact, when I made one for my friend Tim, he ate it over my kitchen sink with sauce oozing out the sides and said, "This is what my mom calls a 'sinky'!" Take some time and care to find the best ingredients you can. There are many varieties of salami, so be sure to ask your friend behind the meat counter at the local grocer for samples, because it's all about personal preference. Pick your favorite, and pair it with Gruyère and a nice crunchy baguette. Curating a sandwich is all about choosing the elements you love. SERVES 2 TO 4 • COOK TIME: 15 MINUTES

Preheat the oven to 450°F.

In a bowl, stir together 5 tablespoons of the mayonnaise, pepperoncini, brine, and hot sauce until combined well.

Without slicing all the way through, slice the baguette horizontally and splay it open. Layer one side with the salami and the other with the cheese. Put the stuffed baguette on a baking sheet and bake until bubbling, about 7 minutes.

Remove from the oven and spoon 2 tablespoons of the pepperoncini mayonnaise evenly over the whole sandwich. Add the marinated onions, drizzle with 1 tablespoon of the marinated onion oil, then layer on the arugula and avocado. Top with the remaining 1 tablespoon mayonnaise and 1 tablespoon onion oil. Cut the sandwich in half and finish off with more mayonnaise before eating.

"If we're not meant to have midnight snacks, why is there a light in the fridge?"
—Bill Murray

6 tablespoons high-quality mayonnaise or Whole30 Mayonnaise (page 286)

4 pepperoncini in brine, seeded and finely chopped, plus 2 teaspoons brine from the jar

2 teaspoons hot sauce of your choice (compliant if you're doing Whole30)

1 demi baguette (about 15 inches long)

¼ pound thinly sliced salami

¼ pound thinly sliced Gruyère cheese

⅓ cup Marinated Red Onions (page 30)

2 tablespoons oil from Marinated Red Onions

½ cup arugula

1 avocado, sliced

teri's favorite chicken salad

GLUTEN-FREE, IF NOT USING BREAD

DAIRY-FREE

WHOLE30

GRAIN-FREE, IF NOT USING BREAD

This is the best chicken salad you will ever have. When my son Patrick was growing up, it was his favorite, and I made a fresh batch at least once a week. Part of the secret to the recipe is blending Peppadew peppers with some of their brine and some mayonnaise to create a Magic Elixir, then finely chopping more Peppadews to create a delicious crunch. It's an absolutely spectacular salad that is loved and coveted by family and friends—who still request this gem on a regular basis. SERVES 4; MAKES A GENEROUS 4 CUPS CHICKEN SALAD • COOK TIME: 1 HOUR

FOR THE CHICKEN

- 3 bone-in, skin-on chicken breasts
- 1 tablespoon extra-virgin olive oil
- 1 teaspoon kosher salt
- ¼ teaspoon freshly ground black pepper

FOR THE SAUCE

- ¾ cup high-quality mayonnaise or Whole30 Mayonnaise (page 286)
- ¼ cup whole jarred Peppadew peppers (about 5), plus ¼ cup brine from the jar

TO ASSEMBLE

- ½ cup finely chopped celery
- ½ cup finely chopped pitted green Cerignola olives (see Tip)
- ½ cup finely chopped jarred Peppadew peppers

Preheat the oven to 350°F. Line a baking sheet with parchment paper.

FOR THE CHICKEN: Evenly coat the chicken breasts with the olive oil. Sprinkle them with the salt and pepper. Put them on the prepared baking sheet and bake for 30 minutes. Remove from the oven and baste the chicken breasts with the juices from the bottom of the pan, then return the pan to the oven and bake for 5 to 10 minutes more, until the chicken is cooked through and the skin is browned and crispy. Remove and let cool.

MEANWHILE, FOR THE SAUCE: In a blender, combine the mayonnaise, the whole Peppadews, and the brine and blend until well combined. Set aside.

ASSEMBLE THE SALAD: When the chicken is cool, remove the skin and set it aside, then use your hands to meticulously pull the meat off the bones, discarding the imperfections like soft tendons, cartilage, and red pieces. Coarsely chop the crispiest bits of skin and reserve to use as croutons on top of the salad. Measure out 3 cups of the chicken, reserving the rest for a different recipe.

continued...

½ cup finely chopped yellow
   onions

¼ cup finely chopped fresh
   chives

1 teaspoon kosher salt

½ teaspoon freshly ground
   black pepper

¼ teaspoon granulated garlic

8 slices brioche, rye, white,
   or wheat bread; crackers;
   tortillas; or grain-free chips
   (such as Siete brand), for
   serving

Divide the 3 cups of chicken into two groups: perfect, moist pieces in one group, and dry, not-so-perfect pieces in another. Coarsely chop the perfect, moist pieces and put them in a large bowl. Put the dry, not-so-perfect pieces in the food processor and pulse for 5 seconds, then transfer to the bowl with the perfect pieces and mix.

Add the celery, olives, chopped Peppadews, onion, chives, salt, black pepper, and granulated garlic to the bowl and toss to combine. Top with three-quarters of the sauce and toss very well to thoroughly coat. If desired, add more of the sauce and mix again to combine. Top with the bits of crispy skin.

This is delicious served on bread as a sandwich, but is also great with crackers, tortilla chips, or grain-free chips, or on its own.

TERI'S TIPS

I fell in love with a vegan grapeseed oil mayonnaise called Vegenaise. It's something that I use for this salad, but feel free to use your favorite high-quality mayonnaise.

I love Cerignola olives and always use them in this recipe. They always come with the pit, so slide your knife around the pit and remove it. If you can't find them, use your favorite high-quality mild green olive.

how to become a spectacular sandwich maker

You take a bit of this, add a bit of that . . . it's the layers that make the magnificence. I've always said a sandwich is only as good as its ingredients.

#1 PROTEIN: Must be fresh. You can make my Roasted Grapefruit Chicken (page 139) or Slow-Roasted Eye of Round (page 184). If you're going to go for store-bought, think honey ham, a rare roast beef, or salami.

#2 CHEESE: I love a sharp ched-dar or Gruyère, but sample something new that would be a unique and delicious complement to your sandwich.

#3 "THE WRAPPER": Always get really lovely fresh bread or a roll. If you are making a Whole30 sand-wich, crisp iceberg lettuce leaves, cut into a "bun," is perfection.

#4 GREENS AND VEGETABLES: Try Boston lettuce, baby arugula, or a nice loose mix of greens. Ex-tra layers of seasonal vegetables like summer tomatoes and ripe avocado or a fresh slaw can take your sandwich to the next level.

#5 SPREAD AND SAUCE: Magic Elixirs anyone? When making a sauce, I like to start with mayo and riff from there—just enough hot sauce to make a beautiful color; ketchup or mustard for taste; and a little bit of something pickled, like a caper or dill pickle. Experiment and play. Stir it up, and spread it on.

#6 EXTRAS: Marinated Onions (page 30) and a drizzle of the oil, pepperoncini, cornichons, marinated artichoke hearts, or your favorite olives will add a final, delicious layer of flavor to finish your sandwich.

salads

I like to say I love salad as a lifestyle, which is perfect considering creating an entrée salad is one of my superpowers. Salad platters are great for a fabulous party as well as a casual weeknight dinner. What's different about mine is that I typically don't toss them. I present them with love and care, on a platter that allows people to choose their favorites. A salad is only as good as its ingredients—fresh, spectacular items make a salad extraordinary. The real secret: Prepare each element yourself. It can take a bit of prep, but you'll wind up with something sensational.

Start with a bed of beautiful greens—whatever is local and in season, both soft and buttery as well as crispy. Salt your greens and sprinkle them with a bit of Marinated Red Onion oil (page 30). Load the platter with blanched, in-season vegetables and a homemade dressing, and don't forget to add elements with unique textures and flavors—think crispy, salty, and creamy. I always like to tuck in a special surprise, like Sweet Potato Crisps (page 288) or Potato Croutons (page 291).

More Tips to Become a Spectacular Salad Maker 102

more tips to become a spectacular salad maker

1. Don't be locked into one kind of lettuce. Feel free to change it up—use an assortment of greens. For a taco salad, use crunchy romaine. When you want something with a little peppery bite, add arugula.

2. Keep your salad seasonal: in the spring, blanch a bit of asparagus; in the summer, add blanched green beans; in the fall, use a cubed roasted root vegetable. And remember you can get a good pear tomato year-round.

3. For a beautiful salad, keep color in mind. I lay out all the components, and assembly is my favorite part. Think of it as an art project!

4. Allow the greens underneath to lead the way. Remember to salt them and add a bit of Marinated Red Onion oil (page 30) before adding the rest.

5. Presentation is everything. For a celebration platter, I'm not about a tossed salad. Create a gorgeous platter separated into sections, and let guests choose.

6. Serving two dressings is absolutely not overdoing it—spooning a vinaigrette over a salad first, then adding a creamy dressing is quite nice.

7. Store-bought marinated artichoke hearts, cornichons, specialty olives, and sun-dried tomatoes are elements that can help pull an exceptional salad together. Finely chopped scallions, chives, and Gomasio (page 36) are great little finishers.

8. Don't be too shy to ask your grocer for samples of produce. Have them cut open a tomato. Try it before you buy it.

TERI'S TIPS

A truly delicious salad involves making every element yourself. Use something like crispy Perfect Oven Bacon (page 294), roasted chicken breast (see page 143) or Slow-Roasted Beef Eye of Round (page 184). Hand-selected lettuces, specialty olives, a blanched green vegetable, pepperoncini, a Jammy Egg (page 292), Smoky Pepitas (page 44), and hearts of palm are a few elements my guests love. If you're not doing Whole30, a bit of sheep's-milk feta can truly be your best friend.

spring greens with salami croutons

GLUTEN-FREE
(IF USING
GLUTEN-FREE
SALAMI)

GRAIN-FREE

It's so exciting when sugar snap peas and asparagus come into season, and this wonderful side salad sure hits the spot. I blanch the vegetables for crunchiness, color, and flavor—it really brings out the green. Served with salami croutons on a bed of arugula and watercress, then dressed with Lemon Chive Vinaigrette, this refreshing salad is a great addition to a barbecue or a buffet, but equally good for a weeknight dinner. SERVES 4 • COOK TIME: 30 MINUTES

½ cup extra-virgin olive oil

¼ cup fresh Meyer lemon juice

2 tablespoons chopped fresh chives

1 garlic clove, chopped

1 tablespoon plus 1 teaspoon kosher salt

¼ teaspoon crushed black peppercorns

5 ounces mixed arugula and watercress

½ cup English peas, blanched (see Tip)

½ cup sugar snap peas (about 2 ounces), blanched and cut into thirds

8 stalks pencil-thin asparagus, halved (about 1 cup) and blanched

½ cup diced salami (check label for compliance if doing Whole30)

1 to 2 tablespoons grated Parmesan cheese (optional)

In a food processor, combine the olive oil, lemon juice, chives, garlic, 1 teaspoon of the salt, and the pepper and process until smooth. Set aside.

On a beautiful large platter, make a bed of the greens, then top with the peas, sugar snap peas, and asparagus. Evenly top with the salami and Parmesan if desired and finish with your preferred amount of dressing, then toss and serve.

TERI'S TIPS
In total, you should use 2 cups of vegetables. If you can't find one of the vegetables I've specified, simply use more of another to get yourself to 2 cups. For instructions on how to blanch, see page 296.

If you're bringing this to an event, get everything chopped and ready to assemble, tote the ingredients to your destination, then plate the salad just before serving.

"You were wild once, don't let them tame you."   —Isadora Duncan

tropical cobb salad
with whole sisters' ranch

Here's a fresh take on the classic Cobb salad. It's full of the usuals, like crispy bacon and avocado, but with mango in place of cheese and juicy, spice-rubbed chicken that adds just a bit of heat. It's cooling, refreshing, and slightly sweet. Drizzle with Whole Sisters' Ranch, and dig in! SERVES 4 • COOK TIME: 40 MINUTES

Preheat the oven to 375°F. Line a baking sheet with parchment paper.

In a small bowl, stir together the salt, hot paprika, black pepper, granulated garlic, and allspice until combined well. Thoroughly and evenly coat the chicken breasts with the spice mixture on both sides. Rub each chicken breast with 1 teaspoon of the olive oil. Arrange the chicken on the prepared baking sheet and bake for 30 minutes, or until they begin to turn golden brown and bubbly. Baste with the juices from the bottom of the pan and bake for 5 minutes more. Remove from the oven and let rest while you prep the vegetables for your salad. Set 2 of the breasts aside for other dishes, then carve the meat from the remaining 2 breasts off the bone and cut the chicken into ¼-inch-thick slices.

On a large platter, assemble the salad, starting with a bed of romaine. Top with the sliced chicken and arrange the tomatoes, avocado, cucumber, and mango in groups around the chicken. Finally add the bacon, marinated onions, and eggs.

Serve with Whole Sisters' Ranch.

*"My religion is very simple, my religion
is kindness."* —Dalai Lama

2 teaspoons kosher salt

1 teaspoon hot paprika

½ teaspoon freshly ground black pepper

½ teaspoon granulated garlic

¼ teaspoon ground allspice

4 bone-in, skin-on chicken breasts (2 for the salad and 2 for leftovers)

4 teaspoons extra-virgin olive oil

8 cups chopped romaine lettuce

1 cup halved pear tomatoes

1 avocado, sliced

1 cup sliced cucumber

1 mango, peeled and cut into chunks

8 slices Perfect Oven Bacon (page 294), cut in half

Marinated Red Onions (page 30)

3 Jammy Eggs (page 293), sliced in half

Whole Sisters' Ranch (page 287)

chicken finger salad
with grapefruit-lime vinaigrette

Chicken fingers evoke childhood and going home. I love to make them when I'm feeling a little bit deprived during Whole30 and I'm ready to enjoy a treat that maybe even feels a little bit naughty. They're hot, smoky, and crunchy, and I love the twist of these served with mixed fresh greens, the fat of an avocado, and the crunch of cucumbers and pepperoncini, finished off with my refreshing Grapefruit-Lime Vinaigrette. While this is technically Whole30 compliant, chicken fingers may not be the best choice for changing your habits during your Whole30. When in doubt, save it for your Food Freedom. SERVES 4 •
COOK TIME: 25 MINUTES

FOR THE CHICKEN FINGERS

1   cup almond meal or almond flour

2   tablespoons hot paprika

1   tablespoon granulated garlic

2   teaspoons kosher salt

½   teaspoon coarsely ground black pepper

2   large eggs

1   pound boneless, skinless chicken breasts

1   cup coconut oil, or enough to fill a medium skillet by about ½ inch

FOR THE SALAD

6   cups soft lettuce, like Boston or Bibb (1 or 2 bunches), or your favorite combination of mixed greens

1¼ cups sliced cucumber (about 2 Persian or other small cucumber)

FOR THE CHICKEN FINGERS: Line a baking sheet with parchment paper.

In a food processor, combine the almond meal, paprika, granulated garlic, salt, and pepper and pulse until completely combined and free of any lumps, about 1 minute. Set the mixture aside in a shallow dish.

In a medium bowl using a whisk or in a blender, beat the eggs thoroughly. Pour the eggs into a separate shallow dish.

Slice each chicken breast on an angle into roughly ¾-inch-wide strips (about 1-ounce slices, or 5 or 6 fingers per breast).

One by one, dredge each chicken strip in the egg, then remove it, letting any excess egg drip off, and gently drop it into the almond flour mixture, coating it completely (see Tip). Handling the breaded chicken as minimally as possible, shake off any excess almond meal and set it on the lined baking sheet. Repeat to bread the remaining chicken strips.

continued...

Line a plate with paper towels. In a medium skillet, melt the coconut oil over medium-high heat and heat until very hot, about 350°F. Working in batches, add the chicken strips to the hot oil and fry until golden brown and crispy, 2½ to 3 minutes, flipping them gently with tongs halfway through (flip them away from you to avoid splashing). Transfer the chicken to the prepared plate and repeat to cook the remaining chicken.

FOR THE SALAD: On a lovely serving platter, arrange the mixed greens. Add the cucumber, pepperoncini, avocados, and bell peppers, grouping each ingredient around the platter until you've filled it to look like a painter's palette. Top with marinated onions and dress it with the vinaigrette.

Pass the platter around the table family-style.

¾ cup jarred pepperoncini (about 8), halved lengthwise

2 avocados, sliced

½ cup diced red bell peppers

Marinated Red Onions (page 30), for garnish

Grapefruit-Lime Vinaigrette (page 58)

TERI'S TIPS

While this recipe requires some technique, it is well worth mastering. For success with this recipe, follow the directions closely but also pay attention to how your chicken fingers are browning in real time. The oil must be hot enough to crisp them, but not so hot that they burn. My tip is to fry one up first on its own as a test to see how long it takes. It's like making your first pancake of the batch: you have to ruin it to get the rest right. And if you have any burnt bits left behind in the oil, skim them out.

When dredging in wet and dry ingredients, I use my right hand for the egg and my left hand for the almond flour, so I never accidentally mix the two.

chicken shawarma salad
with zesty garlic-tahini dressing

GLUTEN-FREE
DAIRY-FREE
GRAIN-FREE

When my kids were babies, I'd slip away once a week with a dear friend for a moms' day out. We'd have chicken shawarma from a little hole in the wall—delivered to the nail salon. The restaurant has since closed, and while my recipe doesn't beat the original, it's still fabulous, and hits all the right notes: tangy, spicy, and oh so satisfying! SERVES 4 • COOK TIME: 30 TO 45 MINUTES, PLUS AT LEAST 8 HOURS MARINATING TIME

8   bone-in, skin-on chicken thighs, deboned if desired

2   teaspoons kosher salt

1   tablespoon smoked paprika

1   tablespoon ground sumac

½   teaspoon ground coriander

½   teaspoon cayenne pepper

½   teaspoon ground turmeric

½   teaspoon freshly ground black pepper

⅛   teaspoon ground cinnamon

1   tablespoon pressed garlic

1   teaspoon finely grated lemon zest

⅓   cup extra-virgin olive oil

3   tablespoons fresh lemon juice

6   cups assorted greens

2   ripe medium tomatoes, sliced

1½ cups sliced cucumbers

Zesty Garlic-Tahini Dressing (page 59)

Marinated Red Onions (page 30)

Place the chicken in a shallow airtight container suitable for marinating. Sprinkle with 1 teaspoon of the salt and toss. Set aside.

In a small bowl, stir together the remaining 1 teaspoon salt, the smoked paprika, sumac, coriander, cayenne, turmeric, black pepper, and cinnamon until thoroughly combined. Add the garlic and mix well to make a paste. Add the lemon zest and stir well. While stirring continuously, add the olive oil, 1 tablespoon at a time, and stir until combined well. Add the lemon juice and mix well.

Pour half the marinade over the chicken, flip the chicken, and pour over the remaining marinade. Using your hands, rub the marinade into the chicken until every crevice is thoroughly coated. Cover and marinate in the refrigerator overnight or for up to 48 hours.

When ready to cook the chicken, preheat the oven to 375°F. Remove the chicken from the refrigerator and let it come to room temperature.

continued...

Arrange the chicken on a large baking sheet in one layer and roast until golden brown and cooked through, about 30 minutes for boneless or 35 to 40 minutes for bone-in.

Remove the meat from the bone, if using bone-in, then slice each chicken thigh into 4 pieces.

Arrange the greens on a platter and top with the chicken, tomatoes, and cucumbers. Drizzle with tahini dressing and top with marinated onions before serving.

TERI'S TIPS

If you prefer a crispier chicken thigh, after roasting, remove it from the oven and baste the chicken with some of the pan juices, then drain the collected fat and juices from the baking sheet. Set the oven to broil and broil the thighs for 2 to 4 minutes more, until browned and crispy.

steak lemon caesar

GLUTEN-FREE
DAIRY-FREE
WHOLE30
PALEO
GRAIN-FREE

This divine entrée salad is great for when you're doing Whole30 and feeling like you need a slam-dunk dinner. It's perfect on a night when I'm feeling a little bit deprived and want to treat myself to something special. There's no better crowd-pleaser than a steak salad: beautiful greens, a lovely dressing, and a perfectly cooked steak. You can ramp this dish up for a party. Use one steak for two people. I love a New York Strip, but it's fun to play around with different cuts of beef, like tri-tip or hanger. Think of this recipe as a template and improv with your own favorites. SERVES 4 • COOK TIME: 30 MINUTES

2   (1½-inch-thick) New York strip steaks

1   teaspoon kosher salt

½   teaspoon freshly ground black pepper

2   tablespoons extra-virgin olive oil

1   head romaine lettuce (about 8 ounces), chopped

12 ounces snow peas (about 3½ cups), blanched for 30 seconds (see page 296)

1   avocado, cut into chunks

    Potato Croutons (page 291)

½   cup Marinated Red Onions (page 30)

    Lemon Caesar Dressing (page 56)

TERI'S TIPS
This is great as a to-go lunch the next day. Make an extra steak and top it with Marinated Red Onions.

Preheat the oven to 500°F.

Using a paper towel, pat the steaks dry. Sprinkle them with the salt and pepper.

Heat a large oven-safe sauté pan (I use a heavy cast-iron one) over high heat until the pan is really hot. Add the olive oil and heat until hot but not smoking. Add the steaks and sear for 2½ minutes, then flip and sear the second side for 2½ minutes. Holding them with tongs, flip the steaks on their edges (the ones with a layer of fat) and sear for 30 seconds on each edge. Transfer the pan to the oven and roast for 6 minutes, or until cooked to your liking (it will cook a little as it rests, too). Remove from the oven and let rest for 10 minutes before slicing.

On a large platter, make a bed of the lettuce, then arrange the snow peas, avocado, sliced steak, potato croutons, and marinated onions in separate mounds on top.

Serve with the dressing on the side.

"When a person really desires something, all the universe conspires to help that person to realize [their] dream." —*Paulo Coelho*

GLUTEN-FREE
DAIRY-FREE
WHOLE30
PALEO
GRAIN-FREE

slow-roasted beef salad

When doing Whole30, I love the idea of a truly delicious roast beef sandwich without the bread. Although you can certainly buy cooked roast beef, this is a genius old-school method to slow-roast an eye of round; once you learn it, there is simply no way you are ever going back. You'll make a juicy roast beef every time, while eliminating store-bought lunch meat. Served with Sweet Potato Crisps, coleslaw, and my Creamy Horseradish Dressing, it's definitely going to make your friends start Whole30 tomorrow. This is also wonderful served with 999 Island Dressing (page 52). SERVES 4 • COOK TIME: 20 MINUTES

FOR THE COLESLAW: In a large bowl, thoroughly toss together the white and red cabbage, carrots, marinated onion oil, caraway, salt, and pepper. Set aside.

ASSEMBLE THE SALAD: Spread the watercress over a large platter. Top with the roast beef, slaw, sweet potato crisps, and marinated onions, individually mounding them on the bed of watercress so that people can choose what they want.

Serve as an entrée platter, with the dressing on the side.

FOR THE COLESLAW

3 cups thinly sliced white cabbage

3 cups thinly sliced red cabbage

1½ cups finely julienned carrots

1 tablespoon Marinated Red Onion oil (page 30)

2 teaspoons caraway seeds, toasted

¾ teaspoon kosher salt

¼ teaspoon freshly ground black pepper

FOR THE SALAD

2 cups watercress

Slow-Roasted Beef Eye of Round (page 184), sliced

Sweet Potato Crisps (page 288)

1 cup Marinated Red Onions (page 30)

Creamy Horseradish Dressing (page 57)

italian chopped salad

How I adore an Italian chopped salad. As a gal who celebrates salad as a lifestyle, there's something about swirling the combination of artichokes, hearts of palm, prosciutto, and sausage in the dressing, with its bits of spice and bite of vinegar, that really hits the spot for me. The grated egg yolk in this version is frankly a stroke of genius. It gives you the kind of richness you need, especially if you're accustomed to adding cheese. It's so satisfying, and easy enough to make for a weeknight dinner. This one is great served with Tomato Salad (page 126). SERVES 4 • COOK TIME: 25 MINUTES

FOR THE DRESSING: Put the vinegar in a medium bowl. While whisking continuously, slowly add the olive oil and whisk until emulsified. Add the Italian seasoning, red pepper flakes, and salt and whisk until combined well. Set aside.

FOR THE SALAD: In a medium sauté pan, heat the olive oil over medium-high heat. Add the sausages and cook, stirring, until golden brown, 5 to 7 minutes. Set aside.

On a large platter, make a bed of the lettuce, then arrange the sausages, prosciutto, pepperoncini, hearts of palm, artichokes, and olives in separate mounds on top.

Top with the marinated onions, the dressing, and the grated egg yolks, if desired, and serve. (Alternatively, toss all the ingredients together in a large bowl as you would a traditional chopped salad and serve with the grated egg yolk over the top.)

FOR THE DRESSING

- ¼ cup red wine vinegar
- ½ cup extra-virgin olive oil
- 2 teaspoons Italian seasoning (check label for compliance if doing Whole30)
- 2 teaspoons red pepper flakes
- ½ teaspoon kosher salt

FOR THE SALAD

- 1 tablespoon extra-virgin olive oil
- 12 ounces precooked Italian sausages, quartered lengthwise and chopped
- 12 ounces romaine lettuce, chopped
- 2 slices prosciutto (check label for compliance if doing Whole30), rolled lengthwise and thinly sliced crosswise into small ribbons
- 12 jarred pepperoncini, stemmed and cut in half lengthwise
- ½ cup sliced hearts of palm

½ cup quartered artichoke
    hearts, sliced into strips

¼ cup small olives, such as
    Niçoise or Kalamata

¾ cup Marinated Red Onions
    (page 30)

    Yolks from 4 large hard-boiled
    eggs, grated (optional)

TERI'S TIPS

If you need more dressing, use the oil from the Marinated Red Onions.

If you have leftover Whole30 meatballs, absolutely include them in this salad.

sugar snap pea and smoky pepita salad

Don't let the simplicity of this salad fool you: it makes a gorgeous, delicious, and impressive first course. The charred hearts of palm, Green Goddess Dressing, and Smoky Pepitas combine for an inspired summer recipe that really feels hearty—it packs quite a punch for a side salad. I have to tell you, I'm a big fan of hearts of palm and if you've never had them charred, it's absolutely worth that extra minute. You're in for a treat. This is great served with Slow-Roasted Beef Eye of Round (page 184), Citrus Cod (page 203), or Not Your Mother's Meat Loaf (page 252). SERVES 4 • COOK TIME: 20 MINUTES

1   tablespoon plus ½ teaspoon kosher salt

2   cups sugar snap peas

2   tablespoons extra-virgin olive oil

1   (14-ounce) can whole hearts of palm, drained

4   ounces butter lettuce

1   cup thinly sliced radish rounds

¼   cup Green Goddess Dressing (page 54)

2   tablespoons Smoky Pepitas (page 44)

TERI'S TIPS
Double the recipe and leave some of the salad undressed to take for a to-go lunch (dress it just before serving).

"A salad is not a swimming pool."
—Patty Turner

Fill a pot with water, add 1 tablespoon of the salt, and bring to a boil over high heat. Prepare a medium bowl of ice water.

Add the sugar snap peas to the boiling water and cook for 1 minute. Drain the peas and put them in the ice water for 5 minutes. Drain again and dry completely.

In a medium sauté pan, heat 1 tablespoon of the olive oil over medium-high heat. Add the hearts of palm and cook, rolling them around, until browned all over, 3 to 4 minutes. Remove from the pan, slice into 1-inch pieces, and set aside.

In the same pan, heat the remaining 1 tablespoon oil over medium-high heat. Add the blanched sugar snap peas and remaining ½ teaspoon salt. Cook, stirring a few times, until the sugar snap peas have begun to blister and brown a bit, 2 to 2½ minutes. Remove the pan from the heat and allow the peas to cool a little bit.

In a large bowl, combine the lettuce, hearts of palm, sugar snap peas, radishes, and dressing and gently toss to coat well. Top with the pepitas and serve.

blt salad

Crunchy, salty, creamy, spicy: This hits all the notes, whether you're doing Whole30 or simply love a delicious salad. If you don't already make oven bacon, it's time to start! It's a game-changer. A summer tomato is a spectacular addition, but during other seasons, change it up with a pear tomato. Grated egg yolks are a genius alternative to dairy, because they add a creamy richness that is so satisfying. Serve on a summer buffet with Green Beans Almondine (page 266), Zucchini Ribbons with Ginger Marinade (page 264), or Spring Greens Salad with Salami Croutons (page 105). SERVES 4 • COOK TIME: 25 MINUTES

Put the lettuce halves on a large platter. Drizzle each piece evenly with the marinated onion oil.

Add 3 slices of tomato and 2 slices of bacon to each lettuce half. Sprinkle the shredded egg yolks over the bacon. Do the same with the avocado chunks. Serve with the dressing.

2 small romaine hearts (about 8 ounces total), halved lengthwise

½ cup Marinated Red Onion oil (page 30)

2 medium tomatoes, each sliced into 6 pieces

8 slices Perfect Oven Bacon (page 294)

Yolks from 4 large hard-boiled eggs, grated

1 avocado, chopped

Creamy Horseradish Dressing (page 57)

TERI'S TIPS

It's so fun to change up the greens and tomatoes depending on what's local and in season. In the middle of summer, use a beefsteak tomato. Other times of year, use pear tomatoes.

tomato salad

I wait all year for a cool, luscious tomato on a hot day. In August and September, I enjoy fresh local tomatoes 24/7 while they are in season. When you're entertaining in the summer, this is an absolute must-do. It doesn't take more than salt to make these beauties shine, so celebrate your farmer for making this deliciousness possible! SERVES 4 • COOK TIME: 5 MINUTES

Slice any large tomatoes into rounds, smaller tomatoes into quarters, and cherry tomatoes in half.

Arrange the sliced tomatoes on a platter. Sprinkle them with the salt and pepper. Drizzle them first with the olive oil, then with the balsamic and red wine vinegars.

2 pounds assorted ripe tomatoes (gorgeous ones of any size)

½ teaspoon kosher salt

¼ teaspoon freshly ground black pepper

1 tablespoon extra-virgin olive oil

1 tablespoon high-quality balsamic vinegar

1 tablespoon red wine vinegar

"You need an entire life just to know about tomatoes."
—*Ferran Adrià*

seafood salad

GLUTEN-FREE
DAIRY FREE
WHOLE30
PALEO
GRAIN-FREE

Oh, how I love a seafood salad. A wonderful restaurant in Chicago, Shaw's Crab House, inspired my Whole30 version. Although you can buy your seafood already prepared, I prefer poaching my own in a magic concoction—I'm somewhat of a lily-gilder and I take it up a notch by serving it with my 999 Island Dressing along with a vinaigrette. I love to make this for Roy on a Saturday, when we sit down with a glass of Sauvignon Blanc and enjoy a leisurely lunch. For a special occasion, serve this with Monie's Carrot Cake (page 259). SERVES 4 • COOK TIME: 30 MINUTES

FOR THE SEAFOOD

16	ounces bottled clam juice
1	cup packed parsley sprigs
½	cup dill sprigs
1	small celery stalk, halved
1	small carrot, halved
1	shallot, halved
	Grated zest of 1 lemon
	Grated zest of ½ orange
8	whole black peppercorns
1	bay leaf
1	teaspoon kosher salt
1	pound large shrimp, shells on, deveined (see page 40)
¼	pound calamari

FOR THE SEAFOOD: In a large pot, combine 2 cups water, the clam juice, parsley, dill, celery, carrot, shallot, lemon zest, orange zest, peppercorns, bay leaf, and salt and stir to combine. Bring to a boil over high heat. Reduce the heat to low and simmer for 10 minutes.

Increase the heat to high and bring the liquid back to a boil. Add the shrimp and cook until pink and just cooked through, 1½ to 2 minutes. Using a slotted spoon, transfer the shrimp to a large bowl and set aside. Add the calamari to the pot and cook until just cooked through, about 45 seconds, then transfer to a separate large bowl. Peel the shrimp and slice the calamari into ¼-inch-wide rounds.

continued...

"Just try new things. Don't be afraid. Step out of your comfort zone and soar, all right?"
—Michelle Obama

ASSEMBLE THE SALAD: On a large platter, start by making a bed with the greens, then arrange the shrimp, calamari, crabmeat, pepperoncini, tomatoes, cucumbers, hearts of palm, scallions, olives, avocados, and eggs in groups on top.

Serve with 999 Island Dressing.

TERI'S TIPS

I'm a two-dressing kind of gal. I love the idea of a light vinaigrette with the greens (see Spring Greens Salad with Salami Croutons, page 105), but the luscious 999 Island Dressing (page 52) is perfect also, so I use a bit of both.

We like the crab, shrimp, and calamari combination above, but feel free to use 1¾ pounds seafood of your choice.

Although it's a bit messy, it's divine if you poach the shrimp with their shells on and then peel them before serving.

I use Persian cucumbers, but if you have larger cucumbers, cut them into smaller pieces.

This can be a great buffet item. You can take it to go by poaching your seafood ahead, skipping the eggs, and bringing your other elements along to toss at the party.

FOR THE SALAD

6   cups assortment favorite greens

½   pound cooked crabmeat

12   jarred pepperoncini

1   cup halved cherry tomatoes

¾   cup sliced cucumbers (¼-inch pieces)

¾   cup sliced hearts of palm (¼-inch rounds)

4   scallions, thinly sliced

⅓   cup Niçoise olives

2   avocados, chopped

4   Jammy Eggs (page 293), cut in half

999 Island Dressing (page 52)

jerusalem salad

This refreshing salad is crunchy, salty, and great with your choice of grilled steak, pork, or chicken. Cucumbers, radishes, and lovely tahini dressing make it a crispy and refreshing meal or Whole30 snack on its own, but it's also perfect as part of a more elaborate dinner. Think of this as a Middle Eastern chopped salad. Finishing it with parsley and my Smoky Pepitas gives it a very Teri twist. My unexpected guests who claim they're not hungry can't resist it. This salad is excellent served with Roasted Grapefruit Chicken (page 139), Cocoa Salmon (page 206), or Cassava-Crusted Calamari (page 222). SERVES 4 •

COOK TIME: 15 MINUTES

- 2   garlic cloves, finely chopped
- ¾   teaspoon kosher salt
- ¼   cup tahini (sesame paste)
- ¼   cup extra-virgin olive oil
- ¼   cup fresh lemon juice
- ½   teaspoon freshly ground black pepper
- 2   cups halved cherry tomatoes
- 2   cups cubed English cucumber (about ½ large)
- 2   cups quartered radishes
- 1   teaspoon finely grated lemon zest
- 3   tablespoons chopped fresh parsley
- 2   tablespoons Smoky Pepitas (page 44)
- ¼   cup drained caper berries (optional)

"The biggest adventure you can take is to live the life of your dreams." —Oprah Winfrey

On a cutting board, use the side of a chef's knife to mash the chopped garlic. When it starts to become juicy, add ½ teaspoon of the salt and mash it with the garlic until combined and broken down into a paste. Set aside.

Put the tahini in a medium bowl and stir until smooth. While stirring continuously with a fork or a whisk, add the olive oil, 1 tablespoon at a time, and stir until the mixture has a creamy consistency. Add the lemon juice, 1 tablespoon at a time and stir until incorporated. Add the remaining ¼ teaspoon salt, the pepper, and the garlic paste and stir to mix well. If the mixture is too thick or not combining well, stir in 2 tablespoons water. Set aside.

In a separate large bowl, gently toss the tomatoes, cucumber, radishes, lemon zest, parsley, and pepitas. Drizzle with dressing to your liking and toss to coat.

Top with the caper berries, if desired. Serve.

> **TERI'S TIPS**
> If you use a cucumber with thick skin, feel free to peel it first. To easily cube the cucumber, quarter it lengthwise, then cut it crosswise into small pieces.

what's for dinner

I have to tell you the truth: I am not an Instant Pot gal. My favorite kitchen tool is the oven, which I say tongue in cheek, but in truth I sort of mean it. I have an affinity for recipes that are slow-cooked over hours, and I adore the magic that unfolds as they do, but here you'll also find dishes that can be done quickly on the stove, and some real crowd-pleasers that are slightly decadent. More than anything else, I want this book to provide people with some great entrées that answer the universal question, "What am I going to eat for dinner?" and that's what this chapter does. It's a daily question that for some can be a daily stress, and I offer some fresh solutions. Not only will you find recipes for what to make for dinner, but you'll get a framework to create your own unique variations. For me, cooking is magic. Let's go!

greek lemon chicken

The Athenian Room in Chicago makes the most fabulous chicken, served with thick Greek fries. Their dish got me wondering if I could create something like it, and inspired me to develop my own. My smoke detector goes off nearly every time I make this, and we all run around turning on the fans and opening the windows, but it's absolutely worth it, and even kind of fun. Nothing can replace their original version, which you should absolutely seek out if you're in Chicago, but this healthful version is soul-satisfying. SERVES 4 • COOK TIME: 50 MINUTES

Adjust the oven rack to 6 inches below the broiler. Preheat the oven to broil. Line a large baking sheet with parchment paper.

FOR THE SAUCE: In a large bowl, add the lemon juice and using a whisk, slowly add the olive oil. Then add the vinegar, garlic, oregano, salt, mustard, and black pepper, stirring well. Set aside.

FOR THE CHICKEN: Thoroughly season each chicken half with the salt and black pepper, then generously rub every crevice with the olive oil. Put the chicken skin-side down on the lined baking sheet and put the pan on the adjusted rack in the oven. Broil for 15 minutes, until beginning to turn golden.

Remove the baking sheet from the oven and flip the chicken over to the other side. Return to the oven and broil for 20 minutes more, or until cooked through, golden brown, and bubbling. Remove the pan from the oven and set the chicken aside. Once cool enough to handle, cut each half into 3 pieces: legs, thighs, and breasts with wings attached.

Arrange the sliced potatoes and lemons on the baking sheet. Return to the oven and cook for 10 to 12 minutes, or until the potatoes and lemons begin to brown. Remove the baking sheet from the

FOR THE LEMON AND GARLIC SAUCE

- ½ cup fresh lemon juice
- ½ cup extra-virgin olive oil
- 2½ tablespoons red wine vinegar
- 1 garlic clove, pressed
- 1 teaspoon dried oregano
- ¾ teaspoon kosher salt
- ½ teaspoon Dijon mustard (check label for compliance if you're doing Whole30)
- ¼ teaspoon freshly ground black pepper

FOR THE CHICKEN

- 1 (4-pound) whole chicken, cut in half
- 1 teaspoon kosher salt
- ½ teaspoon freshly ground black pepper
- 1½ teaspoons extra-virgin olive oil

continued...

oven, put the chicken on top of the potatoes and lemons, and pour ½ cup of the Lemon and Garlic Sauce evenly over the top.

Return to the oven and broil until the chicken is further browned and crispy, about 5 minutes. Remove the chicken from the pan and drain off any excess liquid from the pan (so that the potatoes can cook to a crisp). Return the potatoes to the oven and broil until crisped and cooked through, 10 to 15 minutes more.

Serve the potatoes and lemons with the chicken and the remaining Lemon and Garlic Sauce, either poured over the top or as a dipping sauce.

4   Yukon Gold potatoes, sliced into ¼-inch-thick rounds

1   lemon, sliced into ¼-inch-thick rounds

    Chopped fresh parsley, for garnish

"An alchemist is one who turns everything into love." —Unknown

---

TERI'S TIPS

Every day isn't Saturday, so I've got some great ideas for weeknight eating, too, including a pepperoncini beef stir-fry (page 179), a quick rustic roasted chicken breast (page 143), and some amazing dishes that will please the kids, like potatoes. Some other favorites are Hurley's Spice Rub on a slow-cooked pork roast (page 166) and a Whole30-compliant pork schnitzel (page 171) with a creamy leek slaw (page 60). I have old-world recipes and new ones, and quickly cooked things on the stove. And I like old-school recipes that I update to make new again. I have old-world recipes from Poland, an updated Greek Lemon Chicken (page 134), and spectacular Friday night dishes for your family like chicken potato stacks (page 149). And let's be real: even if you are keeping a more Whole30 kitchen, everyone needs a spectacular pasta in their repertoire (page 224).

sizzling spicy butter chicken

GLUTEN-FREE
WHOLE30
PALEO
GRAIN-FREE

This dish is easy: marinate chicken thighs in a bit of olive oil, garlic, lemon, and red pepper flakes, then sauté and finish off in a mixture of clarified butter and hot sauce, which is a Magic Elixir of its own. The leftovers are amazing alone, or on a salad topped with Marinated Red Onions (page 30) and Smoky Red Pepper Sauce (page 62) the next day. SERVES 4 • COOK TIME: 30 MINUTES, PLUS 2 HOURS MARINATING TIME

1½ pounds boneless, skinless chicken thighs

2 teaspoons kosher salt

1 teaspoon freshly ground black pepper

¼ cup plus 2 tablespoons extra-virgin olive oil

2 tablespoons fresh lemon juice

1 tablespoon finely chopped garlic

2 teaspoons paprika

1 teaspoon red pepper flakes

¼ cup plus 1 tablespoon clarified butter

3 tablespoons hot sauce (check label for compliance if you're doing Whole30)

TERI'S TIPS

For a non-Whole30 version, use regular butter and any hot sauce you like.

Spread the chicken out in a shallow container good for marinating. Season with 1 teaspoon of the salt and ½ teaspoon of the black pepper. Set aside.

In a small bowl, combine the remaining 1 teaspoon salt, remaining ½ teaspoon black pepper, ¼ cup of the olive oil, the lemon juice, garlic, paprika, and red pepper flakes and stir until combined well. Pour the mixture over the chicken, tossing to thoroughly coat. Cover and refrigerate for at least 2 hours or up to overnight, if you have the time.

When ready to cook, remove the chicken from the refrigerator and let it come to room temperature.

Heat a large, dry cast-iron skillet over high heat. Once hot, reduce the heat to medium and heat the remaining 2 tablespoons olive oil. When the oil is warm, add the chicken thighs to the skillet and cook until browned and crispy, about 4 minutes, then flip and cook until cooked through and browned, 5 to 7 minutes more, depending on the thickness of the thighs. Test for doneness. Set the pan aside.

In a small pan, melt the clarified butter over low heat. Transfer the butter to a blender, add the hot sauce, and blend until emulsified. Spoon the sauce over the chicken in the pan, coating the chicken thoroughly.

Serve immediately.

roasted grapefruit chicken

GLUTEN-FREE
DAIRY-FREE
WHOLE30
PALEO
GRAIN-FREE

Here's my spin on an everyday roasted chicken. I've changed it up by using a grapefruit. I will not name names, but I know a vegetarian or two who will sneak a piece, because it is simply so delicious, with its crispy, citrusy browned skin. Part of the trick to this great one-dish meal is the spice blend, which you can make and sprinkle on the chicken in the morning before you go to work—or even the night before. The roasted vegetables absorb the dripping chicken juices as they cook, and there's something about the combination of the chicken fat, spices, and grapefruit that transforms the vegetables. SERVES 4 • COOK TIME: 1 HOUR 50 MINUTES, PLUS AT LEAST 2 HOURS MARINATING TIME

1	tablespoon plus 2½ teaspoons kosher salt
1½	teaspoons freshly ground black pepper
1	teaspoon granulated garlic
1	teaspoon dried marjoram
1	teaspoon paprika
¼	teaspoon cayenne pepper
1	whole chicken (about 4 pounds) (see Tip)
4	tablespoons extra-virgin olive oil
¾	cup fresh grapefruit juice (reserve one of the juiced halves)
3	large carrots, halved lengthwise and cut into thirds
3	cups quartered red potatoes (about 1 pound)
1	medium yellow onion, cut into 8 wedges
5	garlic cloves

In a small bowl, stir together 1 tablespoon plus 1½ teaspoons of the salt, 1 teaspoon of the black pepper, the granulated garlic, marjoram, paprika, and cayenne. Set aside.

Put the chicken on a baking sheet or large plate and coat the skin with 1 tablespoon of the olive oil. Sprinkle the spice blend on all sides of the chicken to liberally and evenly coat. Cover the chicken and refrigerate for at least 2 hours or up to overnight.

When ready to cook the chicken, preheat the oven to 350°F. Line a baking sheet with parchment paper.

Set the chicken on the lined baking sheet.

In a small bowl, stir together the grapefruit juice and 2 tablespoons of the olive oil. Set aside.

In a medium bowl, combine the carrots, potatoes, onion, and garlic cloves with the remaining 1 tablespoon olive oil, 1 teaspoon salt, and ½ teaspoon black pepper and toss to coat evenly. Distribute the vegetables evenly on the baking sheet around

continued...

the chicken. Fold the juiced grapefruit half and stuff it inside the chicken.

Bake the chicken for 30 minutes, then baste it with the grapefruit juice mixture. Return it to the oven and bake for a total time of 80 to 90 minutes (or 20 minutes per pound), basting every 15 minutes. If the chicken becomes too brown, loosely cover it with aluminum foil.

Serve.

"Be yourself; everyone else is already taken." —Oscar Wilde

pork chops and parsnip puree

GLUTEN-FREE
WHOLE30
PALEO
GRAIN-FREE

Juicy pork chops! If you're not there, now is the time! Thankfully, cooking pork well-done is an outdated idea. Try cooking them medium or medium-rare, just like a steak—they'll be juicier and more flavorful. I've paired it here with a delicious parsnip puree, but consider taking it up a notch with some sautéed apples, too. SERVES 4 • COOK TIME: 35 MINUTES

FOR THE PARSNIP PUREE

- 4 cups Chicken Stock (page 47)
- 2 pounds parsnips, peeled and cut into ¼-inch-thick rounds
- 2 tablespoons clarified butter
- 1 teaspoon granulated garlic

FOR THE PORK AND GREENS

- 8 thin-cut boneless pork chops (about 1½ pounds)
- 1 teaspoon kosher salt
- ½ teaspoon freshly ground black pepper
- 3 tablespoons extra-virgin olive oil
- 6 cups greens of your choice (such as spinach, Swiss chard, or kale), rinsed and dried

    Chopped fresh parsley, for garnish

TERI'S TIPS

These pork chops make fantastic leftovers for breakfast with poached eggs and Everyday Greens (page 282).

FOR THE PARSNIP PUREE: In a medium pot, bring the stock to a boil over high heat. Add the parsnips, partially cover the pot, and cook until tender, about 20 minutes. Drain the parsnips, reserving ½ cup of the stock, and return both to the pot.

Using an immersion blender, puree the parsnips with the reserved broth until smooth. Add the clarified butter and the granulated garlic and stir until well combined.

FOR THE PORK AND GREENS: Season the pork chops on both sides with the salt and pepper.

In a large sauté pan, heat the olive oil over medium-high heat. Working in batches if necessary, add the pork chops and cook until well browned on the edges, 3½ to 4½ minutes on the first side. Then flip and cook until done, about 1 minute more. If needed to brown evenly, use a bacon presser to flatten the pork chops in the pan. Transfer the pork chops to a large plate and set aside. Repeat with the remaining pork chops.

Add the greens to the pan and cook over medium heat, stirring, until just wilted, 1 to 2 minutes, depending on the greens you've chosen.

Serve the pork chops on top of the parsnip puree with the greens alongside, and top with any pork drippings from the plate, if you're lucky enough to have them.

pistachio pesto chicken breast

GLUTEN-FREE
DAIRY-FREE
WHOLE30
PALEO
GRAIN-FREE

This rustic dish was the product of my desire to create a simple version of a rolled and stuffed chicken breast. It's far simpler and more flavorful to not-so-neatly slather a roasted, bone-in chicken breast with pesto and serve it with even more pesto on the side. If you have pesto on hand, this is a deliciously simple way to get dinner on the table in 45 minutes. This way of cooking chicken breasts is also perfect for chicken salad or a to-go lunch, so make a few extra pieces. Serve with Sugar Snap Pea and Smoky Pepita Salad (page 123), as well as Green Beans Almondine (page 266) or Everyday Greens (page 282). SERVES 2 • COOK TIME: 45 MINUTES

1   teaspoon extra-virgin olive oil

2   bone-in, skin-on chicken breasts

½   teaspoon kosher salt

¼   teaspoon freshly ground black pepper

4   tablespoons Pistachio Pesto (page 51), plus more for serving

Preheat the oven to 375°F. Line a baking sheet with parchment paper.

Generously rub the olive oil over the chicken breasts to thoroughly coat them, then sprinkle with the salt and pepper. Put the chicken breasts on the lined baking sheet and roast for 35 minutes. Remove from the oven and baste the chicken breasts with the juices from the bottom of the pan. Return the baking sheet to the oven and roast the chicken breasts for 5 minutes more, or until the skin is bubbling and crispy.

Remove the chicken breasts from the oven and top each breast with 2 tablespoons of the pesto, spreading it to cover the breast.

Serve with more pesto on the side.

"I cook the food that I want to eat, and it just so happens that other people want to eat it too."
—*Nancy Silverton*

shoreditch chicken

What I love about social media is the real-time inspiration it provides and how it influences our kitchens and communities. I've had the pleasure of cooking with my British Pakistani foodie friend Freda virtually, as well as together in person in London. Her passion and cooking have inspired this soul-satisfying dish. It's exciting to switch things up in the kitchen, try different flavor profiles, and think about food in a new way. It's not hard to find fresh turmeric, which tastes different from dried and combines well with the other delicious and succulent flavors in this dish. If you don't use sumac and Aleppo pepper, it's time to add them to your repertoire. Serve this with Jerusalem Salad (page 131).

SERVES 4 • COOK TIME: 1½ HOURS, PLUS 3 HOURS MARINATING TIME

In a small bowl, stir together the hot paprika, coriander, smoked paprika, Aleppo pepper, caraway seeds, and sumac. Measure out 3 tablespoons of the spice blend for this recipe and set aside. Save the remainder for another day.

Squeeze the juice from the grated ginger into a bowl, discarding the pulp. Set aside. Do the same with the grated turmeric. (See this technique described on page 296.) Set aside.

Arrange the chicken thighs in a shallow container and sprinkle with 1½ teaspoons of the salt. Set aside.

In a medium bowl, stir together the coconut milk, olive oil, lime juice, ginger and turmeric juices, garlic, and the remaining 1½ teaspoons salt. Stir in the reserved 3 tablespoons spice blend. Set aside about ½ cup of the marinade and refrigerate, then pour the remaining marinade over the chicken. Cover the chicken and refrigerate for at least 3 hours or up to overnight, if you have the time.

When ready to cook the chicken, preheat the oven to 350°F. Line a large baking sheet with parchment paper. Remove the

1 tablespoon hot paprika

1 tablespoon ground coriander

1 tablespoon smoked paprika

1 tablespoon Aleppo pepper

1 tablespoon caraway seeds

1 tablespoon ground sumac

¼ cup grated fresh ginger

¼ cup grated fresh turmeric

12 bone-in, skin-on chicken thighs (about 3½ pounds total)

3 teaspoons kosher salt

1 cup full-fat unsweetened coconut milk, blended

⅓ cup extra-virgin olive oil

3 tablespoons fresh lime juice

6 garlic cloves, chopped

Chopped fresh parsley, for garnish

continued...

marinated chicken from the refrigerator and let it come to room temperature.

Put the chicken, with its marinade, on the prepared baking sheet and bake for 30 minutes, or until starting to turn golden. Remove the baking sheet from the oven.

Without disturbing the chicken, carefully pour the juices from the pan into a small bowl. Baste the chicken by spooning the juices over, then return the chicken to the oven and bake for 15 minutes more, or until it starts to turn golden brown, then baste again with the juices, and if needed, carefully pour off any excess juices once more into the bowl. Increase the oven temperature to 375°F and bake for 5 to 10 minutes, until golden brown and bubbly and the bones of the thighs begin to stick through the skin. If you like the skin crispier, turn on the convection function, or turn up the oven temperature to 400°F if you don't have a convection oven, and bake for 5 minutes.

Pour the reserved marinade into a small saucepan and simmer over medium heat until it has reduced by half.

Serve the chicken drizzled with the reduced sauce and sprinkled with parsley.

"The world is filled with nice people, if you can't find one, be one." —Nishan Panwar

roy's chicken and cheddar potato stack

This is such a good dish—you're going to love it. With stacks of thinly sliced potatoes, pounded chicken breasts, shredded cheddar, and rounds of jalapeño, this was originally conceived as a dinner dish. But in a last-minute move, I served the leftovers for breakfast, and it became a regular on my weekend table. The rest is history. SERVES 4 • COOK TIME: 1 HOUR

1 tablespoon plus 1 teaspoon unsalted butter

1 pound chicken tenders

1 tablespoon plus 1 teaspoon kosher salt

1 pound Yukon Gold potatoes, sliced into ¼-inch rounds

½ cup chopped yellow onion

2 to 3 jalapeños, seeded and sliced into ⅛-inch-thick rounds (½ cup)

½ cup cold whole milk

2 teaspoons cornstarch

¾ teaspoon freshly ground black pepper

8 ounces shredded cheddar cheese (about 2 cups)

1 cup spinach leaves

"Happiness is watching the man of your life cooking for you."
—Unknown

Preheat the oven to 400°F. Thoroughly coat a 9 × 11-inch or 8 × 11-inch glass baking dish with 1 teaspoon of the butter. Prepare a large bowl of ice water.

Put the chicken tenders between two pieces of parchment paper or plastic wrap. Using a rolling pin, pound the chicken tenders until they are flattened to ¼ inch thick.

Fill a medium pot with water, add 1 tablespoon of the salt, and bring to a boil over high heat. Add the sliced potatoes and cook for 5 minutes. Drain the potatoes and transfer them to the ice water to cool. Drain, dry, and set aside.

In a medium sauté pan, melt the remaining 1 tablespoon butter over medium heat. Add the onion and jalapeño and cook, stirring, until soft, about 5 minutes.

In a small bowl, whisk together the cold milk, cornstarch, and ¼ teaspoon of the black pepper to combine well. Add the mixture to the pan with the onion and jalapeño. Raise the heat to medium-high and cook, stirring continuously, until it thickens, 30 seconds to 1 minute. Then add 2 ounces (about ½ cup) of the

continued...

cheese, reduce the heat to medium, and cook, stirring continuously, until the cheese has melted and it becomes a sauce, about 2 minutes.

In the prepared baking dish, lay half the potatoes down as flat as possible. Sprinkle with ½ teaspoon of the salt and ¼ teaspoon of the black pepper. Layer the chicken on top and sprinkle with the remaining ½ teaspoon salt and ¼ teaspoon black pepper. Spoon half the sauce over the chicken in the baking dish (if the sauce has tightened up, don't worry, it will not change the dish). Then add half the remaining cheese and layer the spinach evenly over the cheese. Top with the remaining potatoes and the remaining cheese sauce. Sprinkle the remaining cheese evenly over the top.

Bake for 30 minutes, or until golden brown and bubbling.

Serve.

"Cloth napkins make food taste better, it's that simple."
—Teri Turner

chicken sausage
with fingerling potatoes and broccolini

GLUTEN-FREE
DAIRY-FREE
WHOLE30 (WITH COMPLIANT SAUSAGE)
PALEO
GRAIN-FREE

I adore a one-dish dinner. The combination of sausage, crisp fingerling potatoes, and Broccolini is simply delightful. The trick to getting a crispy potato is to cook them twice, so often, at the beginning of the week, I parcook a couple pounds of potatoes to get them ready for quick weeknight prep and eating. I can't get enough of this dish—it will please your whole family. SERVES 4 • COOK TIME: 1 HOUR 20 MINUTES

1 tablespoon plus ½ teaspoon kosher salt

2 pounds fingerling potatoes

4 tablespoons plus 2 teaspoons extra-virgin olive oil

6 precooked Italian chicken sausages (about 18 ounces total; check label for compliance if doing Whole30), sliced into ½-inch-rounds

5 garlic cloves, pressed

½ teaspoon red pepper flakes

6 ounces Broccolini (about 1 bunch)

2 tablespoons Chicken Stock (page 47), warmed

3 to 4 tablespoons Balsamic Tomato Confit (page 35), for serving

Preheat the oven to 400°F.

Fill a large pot with 10 cups water and 1 tablespoon of salt and bring to a boil over high heat. Add the potatoes to the pot, return the water to a boil, and cook for 10 minutes. Drain the potatoes and let cool. Cut the potatoes in half lengthwise. Set aside.

In a large, heavy, oven-safe sauté or cast-iron pan, heat 1 teaspoon of the olive oil over medium heat. Add the sausages and cook, stirring, until browned, about 5 minutes, flipping them halfway through. Leaving any remaining oil in the pan, transfer the sausages to a bowl and toss with the garlic and red pepper flakes. Set aside.

In the same pan, heat 2 tablespoons of the olive oil with the reserved oil from the sausages over medium heat until warm. Like puzzle pieces, carefully arrange the potatoes cut-side down in the pan, fitting in as many as you can. Season with ¼ teaspoon of the salt. Arrange the remaining potatoes cut-side up on top of the first layer. Season with the remaining ¼ teaspoon salt. Drizzle 2 tablespoons of the olive oil over the top of the potatoes.

continued...

Bake until the potatoes begin to brown, about 40 minutes. Remove the pan and layer the sausage mixture on top. Return the pan to the oven and bake for 10 minutes, further browning the sausages and potatoes.

Toss the Broccolini in the remaining 1 teaspoon olive oil. Remove the pan from the oven and add the Broccolini. Pour the warmed stock around the edges of the pan. Increase the oven temperature to 450°F and return the pan to the oven. Bake for 5 minutes more, or until the Broccolini is al dente.

Remove the pan from the oven and serve topped with the balsamic tomato confit.

crispy chicken bites almondine

I love a great one-dish meal. This one has a fabulous combination of textures and tastes—sweet potato croutons, bits of crispy chicken, sumptuous roast vegetables, and garlicky, salty Green Beans Almondine. The mix of ingredients offers a delicious mouthful in every bite, and little hands (as well as big ones!) will love the size of the pieces. Dig in! SERVES 4 • COOK TIME: 30 MINUTES, PLUS AT LEAST 2 HOURS MARINATING TIME

In a shallow glass or plastic dish or another container good for marinating, mix ¼ cup of the olive oil, the lemon juice, garlic, paprika, red pepper flakes, ½ teaspoon of the salt, and ½ teaspoon of the black pepper until combined well.

Season the chicken thighs with the remaining 2 teaspoons salt and ¾ teaspoon black pepper. Add the chicken pieces to the marinade. Toss to coat well. Cover and refrigerate for at least 2 hours or up to overnight, if you have the time.

When ready to cook, remove the chicken from the refrigerator and let it come to room temperature. Remove the chicken from the marinade and set aside.

In a large sauté pan, heat the remaining 1 tablespoon olive oil over medium-high heat. Add half the chicken pieces to the pan and cook until cooked through and browned, flipping the pieces halfway through, 4 to 6 minutes total. Remove and set aside. Repeat with the remaining chicken (no additional oil is needed).

Arrange a bed of the green beans on a large platter. Top with the cooked chicken bites and then the sweet potato croutons. Serve.

¼ cup plus 1 tablespoon extra-virgin olive oil

2 tablespoons fresh lemon juice

2 teaspoons chopped garlic

1 teaspoon sweet paprika

1 teaspoon red pepper flakes

2½ teaspoons kosher salt

1¼ teaspoons freshly ground black pepper

1½ pounds boneless, skinless chicken thighs, cut into ½-inch pieces

Green Beans Almondine (page 266)

Sweet Potato Croutons (page 292)

TERI'S TIPS
Double the chicken bites to repurpose for breakfast the next day.

southeast asian curry chicken

This dish is just bursting with flavorful spices. I know there are a lot of ingredients, but the reality is, it's absolutely worth it. This dish is all about the prep, but the good news is that much can be done in advance. To keep this dish grain-free, I like to serve it over sautéed bok choy. It's also lovely over rice, and it happens to make fantastic leftovers. Not doing Whole30? Finish the meal off with Gluten-Free Blueberry Crumble (page 79). SERVES 4 • COOK TIME: 1 HOUR

In a large bowl, mix the chicken, the chopped basil, 1 tablespoon of the garlic, the scallions, 3 tablespoons of the coconut aminos, 1 tablespoon of the red curry paste, and the salt until combined well.

In a large skillet with high sides, melt the coconut oil over medium-high heat. Using a large spoon, transfer the chicken mixture, spoonful by spoonful (rather than dumping it in), to the skillet. Using a wooden spoon, cook, stirring continuously and breaking up the chicken as it cooks, until cooked through, about 5 minutes. Remove the chicken from the pan and set aside.

Return the skillet to the heat and add ¼ cup of the warm stock, stirring and scraping up all the bits of goodness from the bottom of the pan. Pour everything from the skillet over the cooked chicken.

In a bowl, stir together the remaining ¼ cup curry paste and 1 cup stock until the curry paste has dissolved. Set aside.

In the same skillet, heat 2 tablespoons of the olive oil over medium heat. Add the onion and cook, stirring continuously, until soft, about 2 minutes. Add the remaining 1 tablespoon garlic and cook, stirring, until fragrant, about 1 minute more. Add a bit of the curry-stock mixture and stir, scraping up any bits of loveliness

2	pounds ground chicken (half dark meat and half white meat, if you can find it)
½	cup chopped fresh basil, plus ½ cup sliced into ribbons for garnish, if desired
2	tablespoons minced garlic (about 8 cloves)
3	scallions, thinly sliced
4	tablespoons coconut aminos
¼	cup plus 1 tablespoon red curry paste
2½	teaspoons kosher salt
2	tablespoons coconut oil
1¼	cups Chicken Stock (page 47), warmed
3	tablespoons extra-virgin olive oil
¾	cup finely diced yellow onion
1	(14-ounce) can full-fat unsweetened coconut milk, blended
3	tablespoons fresh lime juice
1	tablespoon arrowroot starch
1	tablespoon very cold water

continued...

from the bottom of the pan. Add the remainder of the curry-stock mixture and stir to combine well.

Add the coconut milk to the skillet and whisk until everything is dissolved and smooth. Add the lime juice and the remaining 1 tablespoon coconut aminos, then stir to combine.

Make a slurry by mixing together the arrowroot and cold water in a small bowl, then add to the skillet and stir to combine well.

Return the chicken with the juices to the skillet and add the red pepper flakes and cayenne. Stir to combine, and bring to a simmer, stirring occasionally, for 20 minutes.

In a medium sauté pan, heat the remaining 1 tablespoon olive oil over medium-high heat. Add the bok choy and cook, stirring continuously, until the leaves are bright green and the bok choy has released some of its liquid, about 2 minutes.

Plate the bok choy and spoon the chicken curry over the top. Garnish with the basil ribbons and cilantro, if desired, and serve.

2   teaspoons red pepper flakes

½   teaspoon cayenne pepper

4   heads baby bok choy, coarsely chopped

½   cup chopped fresh cilantro, for garnish (optional)

TERI'S TIPS

This makes a lot of sauce, and you will have some left over. Add it to some chicken stock for the beginnings of a great soup. Or pour it over some cauliflower fried rice for a great dish. If the sauce separates, don't worry, it's totally fine and tastes the same.

Feel free to substitute ground turkey or beef for the chicken.

chicken paillard
with pancetta, apples, pecans, and crispy kale

GLUTEN-FREE

DAIRY-FREE

PALEO

GRAIN-FREE

WHOLE30
(WITH
COMPLIANT
PANCETTA)

You are absolutely going to go crazy about this dish, and I'm so excited to share it. Talk about a home run. This perfect autumn dish hits all the notes: sweet, salty, nutty, crunchy. It takes a bit of prep and time, but the combination of ingredients is absolutely fantastic and makes all the effort worth it. Here is a case where rendering fat from the pancetta takes a dish to the next level. I always make a few extra chicken breasts, then put them aside to repurpose for breakfast or lunch the next day. SERVES 4 • COOK TIME: 40 MINUTES

4   boneless, skinless chicken breast cutlets (about 1½ pounds total)

1½   teaspoons kosher salt

½   teaspoon freshly ground black pepper

¾   cup pecans

1   tablespoon clarified butter

2   medium Pink Lady apples, skin on, halved, cored, and sliced into ¼-inch-thick half-moons

¾   cup finely chopped pancetta (a little over 3 ounces; check label for compliance if you're doing Whole30)

3   tablespoons extra-virgin olive oil

2   bunches dinosaur (lacinato or Tuscan) kale, stemmed and cross-cut into 2-inch pieces (about 6 cups)

1   tablespoon chopped garlic

1   cup Whole Sisters' Ranch (page 287), plus more if desired

Preheat the oven to 325°F.

Season the cutlets on each side with the salt and pepper. Set aside.

Spread the pecans out on a dry baking sheet and toast in the oven for about 8 minutes, or until just aromatic. Remove from the oven, coarsely chop, and set aside.

Reduce the oven temperature to 200°F. Put a baking sheet in the oven to preheat.

In a large sauté pan, melt the clarified butter over medium heat. Add the apple slices and cook, stirring occasionally, until lightly browned, about 4 minutes. Reduce the heat to medium-low and cook for 3 minutes more. Transfer the apples to a bowl and set aside. Wipe any remaining fat out of the pan.

Return the pan to the stove over medium-low heat and add the pancetta. Cook, stirring continuously, until the fat has rendered and the pancetta is crispy, about 6 minutes. Using a slotted spoon, transfer the pancetta to a plate and set aside, reserving the rendered fat from the pancetta in the pan.

continued...

Add 1½ tablespoons of the olive oil to the pan and heat over medium heat, stirring to combine with the fat from the pancetta. Add the chicken and cook until nicely browned and cooked through, about 3 minutes on each side. Transfer the chicken to the baking sheet in the oven to keep warm.

In the same skillet, heat the remaining 1½ tablespoons olive oil over medium heat. Add the kale and the remaining ½ teaspoon salt cook, stirring continuously, until well wilted and becoming crispy, about 5 minutes. Add the garlic and cook, stirring to combine with the kale, until the garlic is nicely toasted, about 1 minute. (Be careful! Garlic burns easily and quickly.) Transfer the kale and garlic to a large bowl, add the apples, and toss well.

When ready to serve, remove the chicken from the oven. Spread the ranch dressing over a serving platter, followed by a bed of the kale and the apples, and then the chicken. Top with the pancetta and pecans and serve with more ranch, if desired.

mediterranean chicken artichoke stew

WHOLE30
PALEO
GLUTEN-FREE
GRAIN-FREE
DAIRY-FREE

Here I've created a dish that combines the succulent elements of a stew with the crispiness of a braise. It's a great combination. The olives, artichokes, tomatoes, balsamic, and chicken stock give the dish a Mediterranean feel, and the duck fat takes it over the top. But if you can't get your hands on duck fat, olive oil or rendered bacon fat also work well. SERVES 4 TO 6 • COOK TIME: 45 MINUTES

10	bone-in, skin-on chicken thighs
2	teaspoons kosher salt
1	teaspoon freshly ground black pepper
1½	tablespoons duck fat
1¼	cups Chicken Stock (page 47)
1	(14.5-ounce) can whole tomatoes, with juices
2	tablespoons balsamic vinegar
5	garlic cloves, pressed
1	teaspoon dried oregano
¾	cup green Cerignola olives, pitted and halved lengthwise
1	cup drained canned artichoke hearts, halved (one 14-ounce can)

TERI'S TIPS

This recipe is made with Cerignola olives. They are readily available online or at your local grocery store.

Preheat the oven to 375°F.

Thoroughly season the chicken thighs with the salt and pepper.

In a large Dutch oven, melt the duck fat over medium heat. Add the chicken thighs, skin-side down, and fry until golden, 4 to 6 minutes. Flip the chicken and fry until golden on the second side, about 4 minutes more. When done, transfer the chicken thighs to a large plate and set aside.

Add the stock to the pan and stir to scrape up any browned bits from the bottom of the pot. Bring the stock to a simmer and cook for 2 minutes. Add the tomatoes, crushing them with your hands, then add the juices from the can. Bring to a simmer and cook for 2 minutes more. Add the vinegar, garlic, and oregano and bring to a boil. Reduce the heat and simmer for 1 minute.

Return the chicken to the Dutch oven and cover. Transfer the pot to the oven and bake for 15 minutes. Then remove the lid and bake for 20 minutes more. Return the pot to the stovetop.

Remove the chicken from the pot and set aside. Add the olives and artichokes to the pot and stir to combine. Bring the stew to a boil, then reduce the heat and simmer for 1 minute. Return the chicken to the pot. Serve.

chicken fricassee

This bit of deliciousness is one of the dishes that taught me there's magic in cooking and sharing food infused with love. My early dinner parties had a transformational effect on both me and my guests. That aha moment in my twenties has defined my life. Originally inspired by a recipe in *The Victory Garden Cookbook*, I've updated it with a healthier profile, and it's simply divine. SERVES 4 • COOK TIME: 30 MINUTES

Remove the tender from each chicken breast and set them aside for another use (such as a stir-fry or chicken salad). Season the chicken liberally with 2 teaspoons of the salt and the pepper.

In a large sauté pan, melt 3 tablespoons of the clarified butter over medium-high heat. Add the chicken and cook until browned, 4 minutes per side. Reduce the heat to medium, cover the pan, and cook until the chicken is cooked through, 3 to 5 minutes more. Transfer the chicken to a bowl and set aside.

In the same pan, melt the remaining 1 tablespoon clarified butter over medium heat. Add the carrots and the remaining ¼ teaspoon salt and cook, stirring, until tender, 3 to 4 minutes. Remove the carrots from the pan and set aside with the chicken.

Stir together the stock and arrowroot, then add the mixture to the pan and stir to scrape up any browned bits from the bottom. Add the vinegar and coconut milk and stir to combine. Return the chicken and the carrots to the pan, along with any juices that have collected in the bowl. Bring to a boil. Reduce the heat to medium and simmer for 2 minutes more. Top with the tarragon leaves and serve.

"The only thing I like better than talking about food is eating."
—John Walters

4 boneless, skinless chicken breasts (about 2½ pounds total)

2¼ teaspoons kosher salt

1 teaspoon freshly ground black pepper

4 tablespoons clarified butter

4 cups finely julienned carrots (3 or 4 medium carrots)

1 cup Chicken Stock (page 47)

1 teaspoon arrowroot starch

4 teaspoons apple cider vinegar

2 tablespoons full-fat unsweetened coconut milk, blended

1½ tablespoons chopped fresh tarragon leaves

TERI'S TIPS

For the ideal final texture, slice the carrots into a very fine julienne cut by slicing them thinly with a chef's knife on a wide angle, then cutting the slices into very thin strips.

hurley's special iowa spice rub pork roast

Saturday is the day to get a pork shoulder on the bone and slow-roast it. As an old-fashioned gal, my favorite tool for slow-cooking is the oven. There's no other way to get a crust like this, and no substitute for the magic that happens to this unimaginably delicious, incredibly simple pork shoulder in the oven Use two forks to pull off luscious servings. Perfection. SERVES 6 TO 8 • COOK TIME: 8 HOURS

FOR THE PORK SHOULDER: Preheat the oven to 250°F.

In a small bowl, stir together the paprika, granulated garlic, onion powder, cayenne, black pepper, white pepper, thyme, and oregano until combined well. Set aside ¼ cup for the pork and reserve the remainder for another use.

Evenly season the pork shoulder with the salt. Then thoroughly coat with the reserved ¼ cup spice blend, being sure to cover all sides of the pork. Put the pork on a rimmed baking sheet and bake, uncovered, for 8 hours, or until there's a really deep brown crust and the meat is very soft and fork-tender. After 2 hours, check for fat in the bottom of the pan. If there isn't, add 2 table-spoons water. Baste the pork a few times as it cooks.

MEANWHILE, FOR THE COLESLAW: In a large bowl, stir together the white and red cabbage, carrots, horseradish dressing, mari-nated onion oil, salt, and black pepper until combined well. Cover and refrigerate until ready to serve.

Serve the meat with pan drippings and the coleslaw.

"Work hard, use your common sense, and don't be afraid to trust your instincts."
—Fred L. Turner

FOR THE PORK SHOULDER

- 3 tablespoons paprika
- 1 tablespoon each granulated garlic, onion powder, cayenne pepper
- 2 teaspoons each freshly ground black and white pepper
- 1 teaspoon each dried thyme and oregano
- 1½ tablespoons kosher salt
- 1 (6-pound) pork shoulder on the bone, with fat cap intact

FOR THE COLESLAW

- 6 cups thinly shredded white and red cabbage
- 1½ cups finely julienned carrots
- ⅓ cup Creamy Horseradish Dressing (page 57)
- 1 tablespoon Marinated Red Onion oil (page 30)
- ¾ teaspoon kosher salt
- ¼ teaspoon freshly ground black pepper

alexandra's first communion pork roast with pear sauce

This is such a delight. It's relatively simple, looks like you've fussed, and leaves people licking their fingers. I love when a dish so simple feels so special-occasion. I had this dish at my niece's First Communion, and I had to get my sister's recipe. I literally set it aside, and it became one of those dishes that occasionally played in the back of my mind. When I pulled the recipe out ten years later and made this pork roast, it absolutely did not disappoint. The pear sauce on the side is a bit of magic, and it's scrumptious paired with almost any protein. It's perfect for a graduation, family get-together, or party. Serve it with Green Beans Almondine (page 266) and/or Carrots with Fennel (page 267). Can't wait for you to try it! SERVES 8 • COOK TIME: 25 MINUTES, PLUS OVERNIGHT MARINATING TIME

In a food processor, combine the garlic, parsley, sage, salt, allspice, pepper, cinnamon, nutmeg, coriander, and cloves and pulse until the mixture is broken down to a granular paste.

With a paring knife, make crosshatch cuts in the meat, about 2 inches deep, at 2-inch intervals. Press the spice paste into each cut; if any remains, spread it over the surface of the meat. Wrap the meat in plastic wrap, set it on a baking sheet, and refrigerate overnight or for up to 2 days, if you have the time.

When ready to cook the pork, preheat the oven to 350°F. Remove the pork from the refrigerator and let it come to room temperature.

Transfer the pork to a large baking dish with sides. Bake for 3 hours, or until the internal temperature is 180°F. Remove the pork and deglaze the pan with 1 cup water. Set aside.

Slice the pork and serve on a platter, topped with deglazed juices and pear sauce.

4 garlic cloves

¼ cup packed fresh flat-leaf parsley

6 fresh sage leaves

1½ tablespoons kosher salt

2 teaspoons ground allspice

1½ teaspoons freshly ground black pepper

1 teaspoon ground cinnamon

1 teaspoon freshly grated nutmeg

1 teaspoon ground coriander

½ teaspoon ground cloves

1 (5-pound) boneless pork shoulder, with fat cap intact

Pear Sauce (recipe follows)

pear sauce

MAKES ABOUT 1¼ CUPS

2 garlic cloves, chopped

½ teaspoon kosher salt

5 ripe green pears, peeled,
   cored, and cut into ½-inch
   cubes

2 tablespoons fresh lemon juice

½ teaspoon ground white
   pepper

2 tablespoons extra-virgin
   olive oil

TERI'S TIPS

This is absolutely great
for leftovers. The sauce is
also fantastic with roasted
chicken breasts or even a
steak.

TERI'S TIPS

You will be tempted to get a
smaller roast, but don't—the
leftovers are amazing.

On a cutting board, use the side of a chef's knife to mash the
chopped garlic. When it starts to become juicy, add the salt and
mash it with the garlic until combined and broken down into
a paste.

In a medium saucepan over medium heat, stir together the pears
and ½ cup water. Once hot, cover, reduce the heat to medium-
low, and simmer until the pears are very soft, about 15 minutes.

Transfer the mixture to a food processor or blender and process until smooth. Return the pureed pears to the saucepan and
simmer over medium heat, stirring frequently, until the sauce has
reduced to about 1 cup; the time will vary, but this can take up to
20 minutes.

Transfer the sauce back to the food processor or blender. Add the
garlic paste, lemon juice, and white pepper and pulse to combine. With the motor running, slowly add the olive oil in a thin,
consistent stream and process until the sauce is emulsified. Serve
spooned over the slices of pork roast.

TERI'S TIPS
Buy an extra pork chop and use it to learn the techniques used in this recipe; get a feel for pounding the pork chop and breading it with the cassava flour. It's like making pancakes: you have to ruin the first one. I recommend this kind of experiment whenever you're trying a new technique, like chicken piccata, chicken fingers, or sweet potato crisps.

bone-in pork schnitzel

GLUTEN-FREE
WHOLE30
PALEO
GRAIN-FREE

When I am doing Whole30, I want to create dishes that really celebrate eating, like my spin on pork schnitzel. This dish is so heartwarming and satisfying. There is a bit of technique involved, from the pounding of the pork to panfrying and breading with the cassava flour, which is why I suggest practicing with your first pork chop. It's absolutely worth the effort. Once you learn the technique, you'll have a skill set you can use with fish and chicken, too. Part of the trick is to use one hand for the wet ingredients and the other for the dry. SERVES 2 • COOK TIME: 25 MINUTES

5   bone-in thin-cut pork chops (4 plus 1 for practicing)

1   teaspoon kosher salt

½   teaspoon ground white pepper

½   teaspoon paprika or smoked paprika

2   large eggs, beaten

1   cup cassava flour

¼   cup extra-virgin olive oil

1   garlic clove, sliced into 4 pieces

Old-School Red Cabbage with Bacon and Apples (page 281)

Golden Onion Sauce (page 61)

Creamy Leek Slaw (page 60)

Lay each pork chop on top of a sheet of plastic wrap, then cover with a second sheet. Using a rolling pin (or meat tenderizer), pound the pork chops evenly until flattened to ¼ inch thick, which takes about 1 minute per chop. Discard the plastic wrap.

In a small bowl, combine the salt, pepper, and paprika. Coat each pork chop thoroughly with the spices; set aside.

Put the beaten eggs in a shallow pan. In a separate shallow pan, evenly distribute the cassava flour. One by one, dredge the seasoned pork chops in the cassava flour, then dip them in the egg, letting any excess drip off, then dredge them in the flour again, being sure to coat evenly. Set aside.

In a large skillet, heat the olive oil and the garlic over medium heat. Cook, stirring, until the garlic is golden, about 3 minutes. Using a slotted spoon, remove the garlic from the pan and discard. Working in batches, gently place 2 pork chops in the hot oil and cook until golden on the first side, 3 to 4 minutes, then flip and cook until golden on the second side, about 3 minutes more. Transfer the chops to a large plate and set aside. Repeat with the remaining chops.

Serve with red cabbage, onion sauce, and leek slaw.

lucja's stuffed cabbage

GLUTEN-FREE
WHOLE30
PALEO
GRAIN-FREE

This old-world recipe is an ode to the woman I've had the pleasure of sharing my kitchen with for more than twenty-five years. Lucja originally came to help with my kids, who are now out on their own, but she's still here as a trusted friend and kitchen confidant. She brought this rustic recipe from her home in Poland, and there is a reason this old-world favorite has stood the test of time. The original version was stuffed with rice, but we found that changing it up for Whole30 left it as delicious as ever. The cabbage can be done a day ahead, but this dish is definitely a labor of love, so settle in, take your time, and share this with family and friends. It's one of those meals you will want to eat directly out of the pan.

SERVES 6; MAKES ABOUT 20 ROLLS • COOK TIME: 2¾ HOURS

2	large heads white cabbage, cored
1	(28-ounce) can whole tomatoes, crushed
1	(14-ounce) can tomato sauce
1½	cups Chicken Stock (page 47)
3½	teaspoons kosher salt
1½	teaspoons freshly ground black pepper
1	teaspoon granulated garlic
½	teaspoon dried oregano
¼	teaspoon cayenne pepper
2	tablespoons extra-virgin olive oil
2	tablespoons clarified butter
4	cups chopped brown mushrooms (½-inch pieces)
1	cup chopped yellow onion
3	tablespoons minced seeded red Fresno pepper

Fill a large pot three-quarters full of water and bring to a boil. Put the whole cabbage core-side down in the boiling water and cook for 4 minutes. Flip it to the other side and cook for 2 minutes more, making sure not to overcook it. Using a sharp paring knife, gently remove the outside leaves and stack them carefully on a platter. If some don't look quite wilted enough, note that the leaves will continue to cook when stacked hot like this. Continue boiling and flipping the cabbage, removing the soft outer leaves. As you remove the leaves, any remaining core will begin to stick out; cut it off.

Repeat until you have removed most of the cabbage leaves. At a certain point toward the center, they are really small and not helpful for rolling, but they can be used later to line the baking dish. Set the leaves aside to cool. Once cool, use a knife to gently remove the rib from the center of each leaf, taking care not to puncture or tear the leaves.

Preheat the oven to 350°F.

continued...

In a blender, combine the crushed tomatoes, tomato sauce, and chicken stock, blending thoroughly. Transfer the mixture to a large pot and bring to a boil over medium-high heat. Add 1 teaspoon of the salt, ½ teaspoon of the black pepper, ½ teaspoon of the granulated garlic, the oregano, and the cayenne and stir to combine thoroughly. Set aside.

In a large skillet, combine the olive oil and clarified butter and heat over high heat, stirring to combine. Add the mushrooms and onion to the pan and cook, stirring frequently, for 2 minutes. Reduce the heat to medium and cook, stirring, until the mushrooms and onion are golden in color, 3 to 4 minutes more. Stir in the Fresno peppers and cook for 1 minute. Add the zucchini, squash, 1 teaspoon of the salt, and ½ teaspoon of the black pepper and cook, stirring frequently, until the zucchini and squash are just crisp-tender, about 2 minutes more. Set aside to cool.

In a medium bowl, combine the pork, the remaining 1½ teaspoons salt, ½ teaspoon black pepper, and ½ teaspoon granulated garlic, and the egg and mix thoroughly with your hands (or a spoon). Add the mushroom mixture to the bowl and mix well.

Layer the bottom of an 11 × 14-inch ceramic baking dish with some of the small or not-so-perfect cabbage leaves to help keep the stuffed cabbage from burning. Start filling the best of the leaves: Take a large cabbage leaf and scoop ⅓ cup of the filling into the center. Fold the sides over and roll up from the bottom. Put the stuffed cabbage, seam-side down, in the baking dish. Continue stuffing the cabbage leaves, placing them side-by-side in the baking dish, pressed gently but snugly together, until the dish is full.

Rewarm the tomato sauce and spoon it over the cabbage rolls. Cover the dish with aluminum foil. Using the point of a sharp paring knife, make very small "X" marks in the foil above each stuffed cabbage to allow ventilation as they bake. Bake for 2 hours, or until a fork goes into the cabbage easily. Serve.

2   cups chopped zucchini
    (¾-inch pieces)

½   cup chopped yellow squash
    (¾-inch pieces)

2   pounds ground pork

1   large egg, beaten

"Sharing makes food taste better."
—Marie Rolston
(Kate Shifrin's mama)

fajita steak platter
with avocado crema and smoky red pepper sauce

Practically everyone can agree on fajitas. This pretty version is especially delicious served with my Smoky Red Pepper Sauce and Avocado Crema. Cut the peppers and marinate the meat in the morning so it will come together quickly after work. If, like me, you wind up with spontaneous party guests, you can stretch this dish by adding avocados, salsas, rice, or cauliflower rice, Siete brand grain-free chips, jicama taco shells, or regular taco shells. My version is grain-free, but you can serve this so that there are options for everybody. SERVES 6 • COOK TIME: 30 MINUTES, PLUS AT LEAST 1 HOUR MARINATING TIME

In a bowl, stir together the marinated onion oil, vinegar, salt, and black pepper.

Put the steak in a shallow container and pour the oil mixture over the top. Cover and refrigerate for 1 hour or up to overnight.

When ready to cook the steak, remove it from the refrigerator and let it come to room temperature.

In a large sauté pan, heat the olive oil over medium-high heat. Add the skirt steak (cut it in half, if needed, to fit comfortably in the pan) and sear until medium-rare, 2 to 3 minutes per side (depending on thickness). Transfer the steak to a cutting board and let rest for 5 minutes.

Add the bell peppers and jalapeño to the pan and cook over medium-high heat, stirring continuously, until softened, about 3 minutes. Reduce the heat to low, add the marinated onions to the pan, and stir to combine. Turn off the heat.

Slice the meat into ½-inch-thick strips and arrange the strips on top of the vegetables in the sauté pan. If needed, warm the mixture over low heat before serving. Serve with avocado crema and smoky red pepper sauce.

½ cup Marinated Red Onion oil (page 30)

1 tablespoon red wine vinegar

1 teaspoon kosher salt

½ teaspoon freshly ground black pepper

1½ pounds skirt steak

1 tablespoon extra-virgin olive oil

1 medium yellow bell pepper, sliced into ¼-inch-wide strips

1 medium orange bell pepper, sliced into ¼-inch-wide strips

1 medium red bell pepper, sliced into ¼-inch-wide strips

1 medium jalapeño, seeded and thinly sliced into rounds

1 cup Marinated Red Onions

Avocado Crema (page 221)

Smoky Red Pepper Sauce (page 62)

spicy pepperoncini beef

GLUTEN-FREE
WHOLE30
PALEO
DAIRY-FREE
GRAIN-FREE

This is great for weeknight eating, whether I'm doing Whole30 or just want something delicious. Quick and easy to prepare, it's such a satiating dish. For me, pepperoncini create Whole30 magic. Whether using them in a sauce or adding them to a stir-fry, they give that extra oomph and raise your dish up a level. Here the combination of salty and spicy is elevated by the pepperoncini to create a Whole30 sauce that is an absolute pleaser. **SERVES 4 • COOK TIME: 45 MINUTES**

1¼ pounds skirt steak, thinly sliced across the grain into 3-inch pieces

4 tablespoons coconut oil, plus 1 teaspoon melted

2 teaspoons arrowroot starch

1½ teaspoons kosher salt

½ teaspoon freshly ground black pepper

¼ cup finely chopped shallots

1½ cups thinly sliced yellow bell peppers

½ cup thinly sliced scallions

2 Thai chiles, seeded and sliced into thin rounds

1 cup quartered green beans, blanched (see page 296)

½ cup stemmed and thinly sliced jarred pepperoncini

1 tablespoon pressed garlic

2 tablespoons coconut aminos

2 tablespoons brine from the jar of pepperoncini

1 cup fresh basil leaves

In a medium bowl, combine the steak, 1 teaspoon melted coconut oil, the arrowroot, 1 teaspoon of the salt, and the black pepper. Toss to coat thoroughly. Set aside for 5 minutes.

Heat a large sauté pan over high heat. When hot, reduce to medium-high and melt 1 tablespoon of the coconut oil in the pan. Add half the steak and cook until seared, about 2 minutes. Flip and cook until browned, about 30 seconds. Transfer the steak to a large plate and set aside. Carefully wipe out the pan with a paper towel, then add 1 tablespoon of the coconut oil and repeat with the remaining steak. Set aside with the other cooked steak.

Wipe out the pan and return it to medium-high heat. Melt the remaining 2 tablespoons coconut oil in the pan. When the oil is hot, reduce the heat to medium, add the shallots, and cook, stirring, until beginning to brown, about 30 seconds. Add the bell peppers, scallions, Thai chiles, and remaining ½ teaspoon salt and cook, stirring, until the bell peppers begin to soften, about 1 minute. Add the green beans and cook, stirring well, until warmed through, about 1 minute more. Add the pepperoncini and garlic and cook, stirring, for 30 seconds.

Return the beef to the pan, along with any juices collected on the plate, and add the coconut aminos and the pepperoncini brine. Stir to combine, then reduce the heat to medium-low. Add the basil, stir again, and turn off the heat. Serve.

skillet-seared sirloin

GLUTEN-FREE
DAIRY-FREE
WHOLE30
PALEO
GRAIN-FREE

There is nothing more delightful than fresh asparagus in the spring. As a gal who likes to eat seasonally, I enjoy it with a fervor, from the beginning of the season to the end. Here I've chosen sirloin, which is an amazing, underappreciated cut of beef. It's lean, flavorful, beefy, and a good value. The mix of crisp spring vegetables in a sauce made from a combination of steak and mushroom jus and coconut aminos is delectable. A truly wonderful Magic Elixir! SERVES 4 • COOK TIME: 50 MINUTES

1 pound asparagus

1 pound sirloin steak

2 teaspoons kosher salt

½ teaspoon freshly ground black pepper

5 tablespoons plus 2 teaspoons extra-virgin olive oil

1 pound brown mushrooms, trimmed and quartered lengthwise

2 teaspoons coconut aminos

Creamy Leek Slaw (page 60; optional)

TERI'S TIPS
This is also delicious served with cauliflower rice.

Preheat the oven to 400°F.

Cut off the woody stems of the asparagus. Peel the rough ends and, with your knife at a 45-degree angle to the cutting board, cut each stalk into thirds. Set aside.

Thoroughly season the steak with 1 teaspoon of the salt and the pepper.

Heat a large oven-safe skillet (I use heavy-duty cast iron) over high heat. Add 2 tablespoons of the olive oil, being sure to coat the bottom of the pan. Reduce the heat to medium-high and add the steak to the skillet. Cook until well browned on the first side, about 3 minutes. Flip and brown the other side for 1 minute. Transfer the skillet to the oven and cook the steak until medium-rare, about 4 minutes (or 3 to 4 minutes longer, if you prefer medium). Remove the skillet from the oven and transfer the steak to a wooden board, reserving the juice from the skillet. Partially tent the steak with aluminum foil and let rest for 15 minutes.

Return the skillet to medium-high heat. Add half the mushrooms, season with ⅛ teaspoon of the salt, and add 1 tablespoon of the olive oil, if needed. Cook, stirring, for 2 minutes, then cover and cook until they have released liquid and look shiny, about 2 minutes more. Transfer the mushrooms, along with all the juices from

continued...

the skillet, to a bowl and set aside. Add 1 tablespoon of the olive oil, the remaining mushrooms, and ⅛ teaspoon of the salt to the pan and cook the same way as the first batch.

In the same skillet, heat 1 tablespoon plus 2 teaspoons of the olive oil over medium heat. Add the asparagus and ½ teaspoon of the salt and cook for 4 minutes, stirring once halfway through. Stir again, cover, and cook for 2 minutes more. Stir again and cook, uncovered, until the asparagus is soft and cooked through, about 4 minutes more.

Turn off the heat and add the steak jus, mushrooms and all their juices, and the coconut aminos to the skillet with the asparagus. Stir to combine well.

Cut the steak into ¼-inch-thick slices and serve on top of the mushrooms and asparagus, with creamy leek slaw alongside, if desired.

TERI'S TIPS

Just as some people experience a degree of comfort and relief in wearing a school uniform each day, I feel the same way about my Whole30 breakfasts. I love that I don't have to reinvent it every morning. Quite frankly, I'm always excited to see last night's delectable dinner on a bed of greens, topped with an egg—and don't forget those marinated onions.

slow-roasted beef eye of round

If you've never prepared an eye of round, this genius recipe is going to be a game-changer for you. You will end up with something not only delicious for dinner, but amazing for meal prep. Part of the technique is to cook it on high for a bit in the oven, then turn the oven off and let the meat sit in the oven while it finishes slow-roasting—and under *no* circumstance should you open the oven. This old-school way of cooking it gives you a succulent roast beef that is well worth the wait, and that you will absolutely have on repeat. This is lovely served with 999 Island Dressing (page 52), Pistachio Pesto (page 51), Green Goddess Dip (page 54), or on a buffet with Roasted Grapefruit Chicken (page 139) and Spring Greens Salad (page 105)—it's a party! SERVES 6 • COOK TIME: 3½ HOURS

Preheat the oven to 500°F.

Put the beef in a roasting pan. Thoroughly coat with the olive oil, rolling it around to completely cover. Season the beef with the salt, pepper, rosemary, and oregano. Remove the beef from the pan and set aside.

Set a roasting rack securely in the pan and spread the unpeeled garlic cloves over the bottom of the pan. Pour ½ cup of the stock into the pan, then put the beef on the rack.

Transfer to the oven and reduce the oven temperature to 475°F. Roast for 12½ minutes if you prefer medium-rare, or about 16 minutes for medium. (In case your roast is not exactly 2½ pounds, the calculation is 5 minutes per pound for medium-rare and closer to 6½ minutes per pound for medium.) Turn off the oven and—here's the hard part—do not open the oven door. I tie mine with a ribbon and put a sign on the door that reads, "Do not open." Leave the beef in the (turned-off) oven to slowly cook for 2½ hours more.

1 (2½-pound) beef eye of round roast
3 tablespoons extra-virgin olive oil
2 teaspoons kosher salt
1 teaspoon freshly ground black pepper
1 teaspoon chopped fresh rosemary
½ teaspoon dried oregano
5 garlic cloves, smashed and unpeeled
1 cup Chicken Stock (page 47)

continued...

gluten-free spicy mushroom ragù

Everyone needs to have a pasta dish in their repertoire, and this mushroom dish is fairly simple, while still feeling festive and luscious. Making pasta happens to be one of Roy's superpowers. He does something with a bowl of noodles that is truly a healing art. Part of the trick to taking pasta from good to great is to infuse it with something special. Here we have used a combination of fresh and dried mushrooms. The liquid from the dried mushrooms becomes a Magic Elixir. It's a two-fer: the dried mushrooms infuse the sauce, and the liquid becomes a mushroom broth. This dish is perfect for that Friday night when you've invited hungry friends over for drinks. SERVES 4 TO 6 • COOK TIME: 50 MINUTES, PLUS 2 HOURS SOAKING TIME

2	cups boiling water
½	ounce dried mushrooms (such as porcini, trumpet, or shiitake)
1¾	pounds fresh assorted mushrooms (such as shiitake, brown, and oyster)
1	pound gluten-free fettucine or spaghetti
½	cup extra-virgin olive oil
⅓	cup thinly sliced garlic
⅓	cup thinly sliced shallots
1½	teaspoons kosher salt
1	tablespoon freshly cracked black pepper (the larger size on the grinder)

Put the dried mushrooms in a medium bowl and pour the boiling water over them; set aside to soak for 2 hours. Set aside ¾ cup of the mushroom water and drain the rest, then finely chop the rehydrated mushrooms and set aside.

Slice the fresh mushrooms into nice, big (2- to 3-inch), beautiful pieces and set aside.

Cook the pasta per instructions on the box, then drain it in a colander (do not rinse the pasta after cooking).

Meanwhile, in a Dutch oven, heat the olive oil over medium heat. Add the garlic and shallots and cook, stirring, until fragrant, 1 minute. Add the fresh mushrooms and the rehydrated mushrooms to the pan. Cook, stirring occasionally, for 5 minutes. Add ½ teaspoon of the salt and the pepper and cook, stirring frequently, until the mushrooms have fully released their juices, 10 to 12 minutes. Reduce the heat to medium-low. Add the butter

continued...

to the pan and cook, stirring, until melted, fully incorporated, and creamy, about 8 minutes.

Add the reserved ¾ cup mushroom water, the sherry, and the remaining 1 teaspoon salt and stir until combined well. Increase the heat to medium and bring to a simmer. Simmer, stirring, until somewhat reduced and the alcohol has cooked off, about 5 minutes. Add the Parmesan and stir well to combine. Reduce the heat to medium-low and cook, stirring frequently, until the sauce further reduces and thickens, about 5 minutes.

Add the cooked pasta to the Dutch oven and toss thoroughly with the sauce. Serve garnished with parsley, with more Parmesan at the table.

"If you really love to cook and think that you might like to do it in a restaurant of your own someday, here's my advice: stay home. Have your friends over for dinner and go nuts, but keep out of the restaurant business."
                                                                    —Charles Phan

½   cup (1 stick) unsalted butter, cut into chunks

¼   cup dry (fino) sherry (go ahead and get a nice bottle)

½   cup grated Parmesan cheese, plus more for garnish

    Chopped fresh parsley, for garnish

TERI'S TIPS
Dried porcini is my absolute favorite in this dish, but do not feel limited by that! I've used them all. They key is to soak the mushrooms for the full 2 hours, so you get all the good flavors in the mushroom broth.

seafood

I love cooking and eating seafood, and I absolutely don't shy away from preparing a new seafood or attempting a new recipe. But here's the thing about seafood: we often need a guide. For example, I love lobster, but hate the dirty work. My local fishmonger, Dirk's Fish & Gourmet Shop in Chicago, will cook the lobsters to perfection, separate the meat from the shells and give me both so I can use the shells to make stock, then send me on my way. Your fishmonger can also peel and devein your shrimp. The personal attention is worth paying a bit more. Find a fish shop in your area, because you can absolutely taste the difference when your fish is sold by someone who moves through the fish daily and knows what's fresh and how to prepare it. Making seafood certainly is a specialty of mine, but I couldn't do it without my fishmonger. As a group, fishmongers are some of my favorite foodie friends, so knowledgeable and fun to talk to. If you can't find a fishmonger, the reality is, you can get perfectly lovely seafood at stores like Costco and Sam's Club. We're so lucky to be living at a time when we have so many options available.

If pressed, I can separate people into two categories: those who love seafood and those who just think they don't. If you fall into that second category, unless you're allergic, I challenge you to suspend your idea that you're not a seafood person and try one of these recipes. It's absolutely imperative to try new dishes and stay out of a cooking rut—it keeps you inspired in the kitchen and happy in life—even if you think you don't like seafood.

spicy shrimp on creamy mashed potatoes

This unexpected combination of rustic smashed potatoes and spicy shrimp is rich and delicious—kind of homestyle. We've changed it up by leaving the skin on the potatoes. When topped with spicy, succulent shrimp in my homemade tomato sauce, it becomes truly divine and will have you reaching for seconds before you've finished your first bite. I prefer it spicy, but feel free to cut the quantity of red pepper flakes in half. This lighter Whole30 version is absolutely delectable and the perfect mouthful. SERVES 4 • COOK TIME: 50 MINUTES

Preheat the oven to 175°F.

Fill a medium pot with water, add 1 tablespoon of the salt, and bring to a boil over high heat. Add the potatoes and boil until soft, about 20 minutes. Drain the potatoes and transfer them to a large bowl.

Add 1½ teaspoons of the salt and 3 tablespoons of the clarified butter to the bowl with the potatoes and smash and mix using a potato masher. Add the stock and stir to combine. Cover the potatoes and transfer to the oven to keep warm.

Heat a large sauté pan over medium heat. Dry-roast the red pepper flakes in the pan for just a few seconds, then add the black pepper and dry-roast it for a few seconds, or until fragrant. Add the olive oil and 1 tablespoon of the clarified butter and cook, stirring, until the butter has melted and combined with the oil and spices. Add the shallots and 1 teaspoon of the salt. Stir to combine and cook, stirring, until the shallots are translucent,

continued...

1	tablespoon plus 3½ teaspoons kosher salt
2	pounds small white potatoes
7	tablespoons clarified butter
¾	cup Chicken Stock (page 47)
1 to 2	teaspoons red pepper flakes, per desired heat level
1	tablespoon coarsely ground black pepper
1	tablespoon extra-virgin olive oil
¼	cup plus 2 tablespoons chopped shallots
2	pounds cherry tomatoes, halved (seems like a lot, but they cook down!)
1	(8-ounce) jar clam juice
1	pound rock shrimp or small wild-caught shrimp, peeled and deveined (if possible)
	Chopped fresh parsley, for garnish (optional)

1 to 2 minutes. Add the tomatoes and clam juice and stir to combine. Cook for 10 minutes, then reduce the heat to medium-low and simmer until the tomatoes break down to form a luscious sauce, 15 to 20 minutes, depending on how firm your tomatoes are.

Add the remaining 3 tablespoons clarified butter and stir to combine. Add the shrimp and remaining 1 teaspoon salt and cook, stirring occasionally, until the shrimp are just cooked through, about 3 minutes.

Spoon the potatoes onto a plate. Top with the shrimp and tomato sauce and serve garnished with parsley, if desired.

"I've been absolutely terrified every moment of my life—and I've never let it keep me from doing a single thing I wanted to do."   —Georgia O'Keeffe

TERI'S TIPS

If you can't find rock shrimp, use small shrimp. The dish can be made better by leaving the shrimp in the shells and peeling after. It's a bit of a hassle, but is absolutely delicious. If you are not doing Whole30, use regular butter. After 25 minutes, if the tomatoes aren't broken down enough, take a fork and poke them!

shrimp pad thai

Who doesn't love pad Thai—and this one is Whole30 to boot. I am absolutely delighted with my spin on this favorite. Here I've used barely sautéed shrimp on a bed of thinly sliced cabbage and julienned carrots. Sprinkled with roasted cashews, scallions, and a squeeze of lime, then topped with the yummiest Spicy Almond Sauce, it's a crowd-pleaser. The leftovers are great, but you're not likely to have any.

SERVES 4 • COOK TIME: 30 MINUTES

FOR THE SHRIMP

- 1 tablespoon extra-virgin olive oil
- 1 tablespoon hot sauce (check label for compliance if doing Whole30)
- ½ teaspoon finely grated lemon zest
- ½ teaspoon kosher salt
- ¼ teaspoon freshly ground black pepper
- ¼ teaspoon cayenne pepper
- 1 pound large shrimp, peeled and deveined
- 1 teaspoon paprika
- 1 tablespoon coconut oil

FOR THE VEGETABLES

- 1 tablespoon coconut oil
- ¾ cup chopped yellow onion
- 2 tablespoons chopped garlic
- 3 cups finely julienned carrots
- 2 teaspoons kosher salt
- ¼ teaspoon freshly ground black pepper

FOR THE SHRIMP: In a large bowl, mix the olive oil, hot sauce, lemon zest, salt, black pepper, and cayenne until combined well. Add the shrimp to the bowl and toss to thoroughly coat. Let marinate for 5 minutes. Add the paprika and toss to coat the shrimp.

In a large skillet, melt the coconut oil over medium-high heat. Add the shrimp to the pan and cook, turning gently, until pink and just cooked through, about 3 minutes; be sure not to overcook. Transfer the shrimp to a bowl and set aside.

FOR THE VEGETABLES: In the same pan, melt the coconut oil. Add the onion and garlic and cook, stirring, until translucent, about 1 minute. Add the carrots, 1 teaspoon of the salt, and the black pepper and cook, stirring, until tender, about 1½ minutes. Add the cabbage and the remaining 1 teaspoon salt and cook, stirring and rotating the ingredients from the bottom of the pan to the top, until the cabbage is softened and melds well with the carrots, 2 to 2½ minutes.

continued...

4   cups thinly sliced cabbage

¾   cup thinly sliced scallions

½   cup Stir-Fry Infuser (page 49)

½   cup chopped roasted cashews

1   lime, cut into wedges, for serving

    Spicy Almond Sauce (page 63), for serving

Add the scallions, stir-fry infuser, and cashews and stir to combine; cook for 30 seconds. Return the shrimp and any juices from the bowl to the pan and stir to combine and warm through.

Serve with limes wedges and spicy almond sauce alongside.

citrus cod with sautéed spinach

GLUTEN-FREE
WHOLE30
PALEO
GRAIN-FREE

This is a wonderful and simple dish for a weeknight. It's fast and easy. Citrus, capers, spinach, and baby tomatoes are key to the light and luscious sauce. Although this is delicious for a Tuesday-night dinner, you'll want to be eating it on the other six nights of the week, I'm sure. SERVES 4 • COOK TIME: 25 MINUTES

2½ teaspoons kosher salt, plus a pinch

1 teaspoon freshly ground black pepper

1 teaspoon finely grated lemon zest

4 (6-ounce) pieces cod

½ cup almond meal, for dusting

¼ cup extra-virgin olive oil

1 cup quartered grape or cherry tomatoes

¼ cup clarified butter

1 tablespoon fresh lemon juice

1 tablespoon fresh orange juice

1 tablespoon coconut aminos

1 tablespoon capers

2 tablespoons Chicken Stock (page 47)

2 cups chopped spinach

"Be thankful for what you have; you'll end up having more."
—Oprah Winfrey

Preheat the oven to 200°F.

In a small bowl, stir together the salt, black pepper, and lemon zest. Set aside.

Pat the cod dry with a paper towel. Sprinkle each piece thoroughly with the spice blend, then dust them on all sides with the almond meal.

In a large sauté pan, heat the olive oil over medium-high heat. Add the cod to the pan, then immediately reduce the heat to medium. Cook the cod until golden and just cooked through, about 3 minutes per side, or a bit longer for thicker pieces. Transfer the fish to a baking sheet and put it in the oven to keep warm.

Wipe out the pan and set it over medium heat. Combine the tomatoes, clarified butter, lemon juice, orange juice, coconut aminos, capers, and a pinch of salt in the pan, stir, and bring to a boil. Reduce the heat to medium and simmer until the tomatoes begin to soften, about 1 minute. Add the spinach and the stock and cook, stirring to combine well, until the spinach has wilted, about 1 minute.

continued...

Remove the fish from the oven. Use some of the spinach and the tomatoes from the sauce as a base on each serving plate. Then put the cod pieces on the spinach and tomatoes and top with the sauce to serve.

TERI'S TIPS

Cod can vary greatly in thickness, so you may need to adjust the cooking time of this dish slightly. And keep in mind that the thicker the piece of fish, the better it holds together.

Cooking with almond meal can also be tricky, as it can burn very easily. Never get your pan too hot, and watch your almond meal very closely.

Your dish is only as good as your ingredients, so for delicious seafood, always start with excellent product.

"Chefs are at the end of a long chain of individuals who work hard to feed people. Farmers, beekeepers, bakers, scientists, fishermen, grocers, we are all part of that chain, all food people, all dedicated to feeding the world."
—José Andrés

sweet-and-sour fish

I've long loved sweet-and-sour fish, but the trick is to make it just as delicious without a sugary sauce. With flavors like orange juice, red curry paste, citrus, and mango on a bed of crisp julienned carrots, my updated version is absolutely delectable. If you're not doing Whole30 and are looking for a hack to take this dish out of the stratosphere, then add a small jar of baby corn in vinegar brine, with a healthy splash of the brine from the jar. It's a spectacular finish. SERVES 4 • COOK TIME: 20 MINUTES

- 4 (6-ounce) red snapper fillets
- 1 teaspoon kosher salt
- ½ teaspoon freshly ground black pepper
- ½ teaspoon ground coriander
- ½ teaspoon ground ginger
- ¼ cup extra-virgin olive oil
- 3 medium carrots, finely julienned
- 6 garlic cloves, pressed
- ½ cup fresh orange juice
- 1 tablespoon red curry paste
- 2 tablespoons pureed mango
- 2 tablespoons coconut aminos
- 2 tablespoons fresh lemon juice
- 1 tablespoon fresh lime juice

TERI'S TIPS
If not doing Whole30, serve with rice.

Preheat the oven to warm.

Season each piece of fish with the salt and black pepper. Then season with the coriander and ginger.

In a large sauté pan, heat the olive oil over high heat. When the oil is warm, reduce the heat to medium. Add the fish to the pan, skin-side down, and cook until just cooked through, turning once, about 6 minutes total (or longer, if your fillets are on the thicker side). Transfer the fish to an oven-safe plate and keep warm in the oven.

In the same pan, cook the carrots and garlic over medium-high heat, stirring and scraping the bottom of the pan to loosen the fish bits, until brown and caramelized, about 3 minutes. Reduce the heat to medium.

In a medium bowl, stir together the orange juice and red curry paste. Add the mixture to the pan and stir. Add the mango puree, coconut aminos, lemon juice, and lime juice and cook, stirring to combine well, until thoroughly warmed.

To serve, scoop some of the carrots out of the sauce to use as the base on your plate. Put the fish on top of the carrots and spoon the sauce over.

cocoa salmon

This is a standout. It might seem counterintuitive, but adding cocoa is the Magic Elixir here. This combination of savory spices with unsweetened cocoa creates a crispy barbecue finish, leaving the salmon so moist, it absolutely melts in your mouth. **SERVES 4 • COOK TIME: 15 MINUTES**

Heat a grill to medium-high.

In small bowl, stir together the sugar, paprika, chili powder, salt, cocoa powder, mustard, black pepper, and cayenne until combined thoroughly. Reserve 3 tablespoons for this recipe and set the rest aside for another use.

Using a pastry brush, brush the salmon with the oil to thoroughly coat all sides. Sprinkle the 3 tablespoons of spice blend evenly over the salmon, using about 2 teaspoons per piece and coating them well. Let rest for 5 minutes.

Put the fillets on the grill and cook until just cooked through, about 3 minutes each side, or until done to your liking. Serve with Green Beans Almondine (page 266).

"The most revolutionary thing a woman can do is not explain herself."
                        —Glennon Doyle

2	tablespoons cane sugar
1	tablespoon paprika
1	tablespoon chili powder
1	teaspoon kosher salt
2	teaspoons unsweetened cocoa powder
1	teaspoon dry mustard
1	teaspoon freshly ground black pepper
¼	teaspoon cayenne pepper
4	(6-ounce) pieces salmon
3	tablespoons extra-virgin olive oil

TERI'S TIPS

Always clean and oil your grill before using.

This is great for leftovers and for a to-go lunch the next day.

Master this, and you will have a great dinner party dish.

pot sticker fish cakes

I love pot stickers. (Actually, who doesn't?) Rather than missing out on something because it isn't Whole30-compliant, I decided to get into the kitchen and turn the traditional notion of pot stickers inside out. Full of delicious flavor and gluten-free, these are absolutely mouth-watering. Having a neighborhood dinner party? Serve them with my Asian Steak Salad (page 115)! What's the magic word? More, please. SERVES 4; MAKES 7 OR 8 CAKES • COOK TIME: 1 HOUR

In a food processor, combine the shrimp and fish and pulse for just 3 seconds, making sure to keep them somewhat chunky so the fish cakes hold together when cooked (see Tip). Transfer the mixture to a medium bowl.

Add the greens beans, scallions, carrots, ginger juice, lemongrass, egg, coconut aminos, white pepper, and salt and mix to combine well with the seafood. Using a food scale, make 3-inch patties weighing 3 ounces each. Set aside.

In a large stainless steel skillet, heat the olive oil over medium to medium-low heat. Working in batches if needed, add the fish patties to the hot oil and fry until a golden brown crust forms on the bottom, about 4 minutes. Gently flip the patties and fry for 1 minute, then cover the pan and cook the patties until the shrimp is cooked through in the middle, about 3 minutes more. Remove from the heat and set aside.

For each serving, put some of the sugar snap peas in a bowl and top with 2 fish cakes. Serve with dipping sauce on the side, if desired.

Tools: kitchen scale

1 pound shrimp, peeled and deveined

½ pound white-fleshed fish, such as cod, haddock, or halibut

¾ cup finely chopped green beans

¾ cup thinly sliced scallions

¾ cup diced carrots

Juice from 3 tablespoons grated fresh ginger (see page 296)

3 tablespoons finely chopped lemongrass

1 large egg, beaten

1½ tablespoons coconut aminos

½ teaspoon ground white pepper

1½ teaspoons kosher salt

2 tablespoons extra-virgin olive oil

2 cups sugar snap peas, blanched (page 296)

Dipping Sauce (page 49), optional

TERI'S TIPS

A gluten-free fish cake needs to have a lot of texture to hold together. If you overprocess the fish and shrimp in the food processor, the cake won't hold together, so be sure to leave the fish and shrimp in chunks.

a day in the life

It starts with a ding in the dark . . . that brings a glow into the room. And while most others are still in deep sleep, Teri's day begins. Five minutes after opening her eyes, she has already sent twenty-four direct messages to followers and friends already awake in various time zones, replied to the sixteen texts that arrived in the middle of the night, thought of ten ways to make a recipe Whole30-compliant and improve other people's lives and contacted everyone who might want to pitch in, and mentally written her shopping list, all while somehow making the best breakfast you've ever had.

Dropping into Teri's life is a bit like jumping into a car that is already moving, or, as Teri would say, "It's kind of like a slippery pig . . . hard to get ahold of." Hopping in mid-ride on one of those wonderful days when she has created a new concoction, two new Magic Elixirs, and found a new variety of cucumber at the farmers' market is the best . . .

One moment she is discussing how to make a Whole30 version of a romesco sauce, when all of a sudden she bursts out, "There's my mom! Oh, she's saying hello! Look, Laurie, there's my mom!" So Patty Turner is here, too, floating gently through the backyard in the form of a butterfly. Moments later, she's on the phone with the potter, discussing Marinated Red Onion bowls, but Patrick texts, so she tells the potter she'll call her back and then calls Patrick, because he and Lucy come first, whether they are excitedly talking about their careers, moving into a new space, getting a haircut, or picking out the perfect tomato at the farmers' market. While talking to Patrick, she smiles and stirs the romesco sauce. Teri's kitchen is the hub of her home. It, along with her kids, family, and close friends, is the heartbeat. When you walk in, all your senses are engaged.

Zach and Teri. Teri and Zach. Writing. Photographing. Filming. Making calls. Answering doors. Laughing in the kitchen. Preparing. Planning. Fine-tuning. Finishing each other's sentences. Are the knives sharpened? Tim arrives for the book shoot, arms loaded with props. A huddle follows: *How best to shoot this Zucchini Frittata? Natural light? Which angle? Voiceover? Let's shoot it from above!* There's chopping, and the ring of the oven timer, and they mean it when they say if you can't stand the heat, get out of the kitchen, because it's getting hot in here. This is exciting. It is invigorating. This is love. The smell of the magic that is being created on the stove, the sizzling sounds and timers going off as a reminder to flip the salmon cakes. (If only the smell of all this magic could be bottled!) A timer pings, and this is all the music Teri needs. This is the symphony of No Crumbs Left and Teri's life. She takes everything she does very seriously, but with a smile; she has boundless energy and, of course, a phone or two in her hand. She adores keeping in touch. She loves what she does. It's contagious.

Suddenly, the beeping and chirping of the smoke alarm punctuates an Instagram story, and Teri gleefully incorporates it while everyone else jumps into action, fanning and fanning; we know what to do, so we fan, with dish towels and newspapers and cookie sheets, sweeping out the excess smoke.

The smoke detector quiets, but the dings, pings, and rings continue. An Instagram post goes up—onion bowls! They're back! And they're selling like hotcakes. Teri is giving one away to a follower this second. A buzz! Lucy has texted her new headshot photos, and Teri's smile grows. They hop on the phone to discuss. Then the romesco is ready to taste, and we jump at the chance. *More salt? More pepper?* Nope. It's perfect, we all agree. *Oh! Let's film it.*

Roy calls, they check in, then she asks which seafood he thinks will go best with the pasta dish they're working on. "Shrimp? Clams? Mussels? Lobster? Hmmmm."

They say if you want to get something done, ask a busy person to do it. And with many balls in the air, Teri makes it look easy. She wonders aloud, "Which platter to use for a salad photo for the book?" then gets on a call with a follower and listens intently, talking her through how to make a Whole30 mayo, as she sautés the meat for what will become Spicy Pepperoncini Beef. Suddenly a timer and the doorbell ring at the same time. Ten seconds later another timer goes off and everyone looks around, wondering what needs to be flipped or turned off. "Was that two minutes? Hi, Kate!" Teri says, knowing exactly what she was timing, and why the neighbor is walking in. They spend a few minutes catching up, and moments later, as Kate is leaving— almost out the door, her arms loaded with a few stuffed to-go containers of freshly made roast chicken breast and a mason jar filled with cashew crema—Teri yells, "Oh, and take some greens, fresh from the farmers' market!" It's Teri's passion, her calling, her superpower! Her well-equipped kitchen may be where the "work" takes place, but Teri's reach extends far beyond its confines. Nothing goes to waste in this kitchen, no one leaves Teri's house empty-handed, and no matter how you felt before you arrived, you're now simply happier.

This is how Teri feeds her soul. This is her umami. Another ding. This time it's a DM from a loyal follower's boyfriend; he is about to propose and wants Teri's help. Will she make a special proposal post to help him? Of course. She records a couple of proposal messages before she's satisfied, and while she's waiting for the correct time to send the message, she comments on an Instagram post and OKs a frittata photo that is about to be posted, and she and Zach start discussing the when and where of the next No Crumbs Left meet-up. And by the way, the answer to the proposal was yes! Because, if not now, when? And . . . repeat. Happily repeat.

—*Laurice Bell*

sea scallops with orange-tarragon sauce

Scallops are totally delicious and need only a quick sear for the best result. The fresh mixture of citrus with clarified butter and tarragon is a perfect marriage of flavors that gently coats, but doesn't overwhelm, the scallops for a succulent bite with each forkful. SERVES 4 • COOK TIME: 20 MINUTES

Rinse the scallops in cold water, then place between two towels and let dry for 10 minutes. When the scallops are completely dry, season them with ⅛ teaspoon of the salt and the pepper. Set aside.

In a small saucepan, melt 5 tablespoons of the clarified butter over medium-low heat. Add the garlic and stir, cooking for 1 minute until fragrant. Add the orange zest, orange juice, tarragon, and remaining ¼ teaspoon salt and stir to combine. Remove from the heat and set aside.

In a medium cast-iron pan, melt the remaining 1 tablespoon clarified butter over high heat. Reduce the heat to medium-high and add the scallops to the pan. Cook until lightly browned on the bottom, about 2½ minutes. Flip to the other side and cook until just cooked through, about 1½ minutes more. Transfer the scallops to a serving dish and set aside.

Pour the mixture from the small saucepan into the skillet. Warm the sauce over low heat, stirring and scraping up any caramelized bits from the bottom of the pan, for 30 seconds, then pour the sauce over the scallops.

Serve immediately.

1 pound large sea scallops

⅛ teaspoon plus ¼ teaspoon kosher salt

⅛ teaspoon freshly ground black pepper

6 tablespoons clarified butter

1 teaspoon finely grated orange zest

3 tablespoons fresh orange juice

1 teaspoon finely chopped garlic

1 tablespoon minced fresh tarragon leaves

TERI'S TIPS
The key to browning the scallops is to make sure they are completely dry before cooking.

tuna, watermelon, and jicama bites with avocado crema

Here's something unique: using jicama, I created an appetizer that is Whole30-compliant with all the crunchy satisfaction of a tortilla chip. If you haven't discovered jicama as a grain-free chip, you might want to get going on that. Topping the crisp jicama, juicy watermelon, and sushi-grade tuna with Avocado Crema makes this a refreshing and delicious summer treat or weeknight dinner. SERVES 4 •

COOK TIME: 30 MINUTES

1   cup cubed watermelon (½-inch pieces)

1   cup cubed sushi-grade fresh tuna (about 12 ounces; ½-inch pieces)

2   tablespoons finely chopped red Fresno pepper (about 1 medium)

½   teaspoon salt, plus more as needed

1   teaspoon fresh lime juice

1   teaspoon extra-virgin olive oil

¼   teaspoon freshly ground black pepper

    Avocado Crema (recipe follows)

1   jicama, peeled, quartered, and cut into 20 ⅛-inch-thick slices

½   avocado, cut into 20 slices

    Fresh cilantro leaves, for garnish

1   lime, cut into wedges

In a medium bowl, combine the watermelon, tuna, Fresno pepper, and salt and toss gently to combine. Set aside.

In a separate small bowl, stir together the lime juice, olive oil, and black pepper. Pour the mixture over the tuna-watermelon mixture and gently toss to combine. Cover with plastic wrap and refrigerate for 20 minutes.

When ready to serve, remove the tuna from the refrigerator. Evenly spread 1 teaspoon of the avocado crema on each slice of jicama, all the way to the edges. Spoon 1 heaping tablespoon of the tuna mixture on top and add a slice of avocado.

Garnish with a cilantro leaf, a squeeze of lime juice, and a sprinkle of salt, if needed. Serve immediately.

> **TERI'S TIPS**
> This is a great appetizer, but is also wonderful served as a weeknight dinner.

"If you get tired, learn to rest, not to quit." —Banksy

avocado crema

1 medium avocado
(about 8 ounces)

½ cup coarsely chopped fresh
cilantro

¼ cup Whole30 Mayonnaise
(page 286)

1 tablespoon fresh lime juice

½ teaspoon kosher salt

In a food processor, combine the avocado, cilantro, mayonnaise, lime juice, and salt and process until smooth.

cassava-crusted calamari

My intention with this recipe was to create a more healthful fried calamari that's grain-free, and this wonderful Whole30 version is totally satisfying. Here I've paired it with my revolutionary 999 Island Dressing. It's hard to have just one. SERVES 4 • COOK TIME: 20 MINUTES

Preheat the oven to 200°F. Line a baking sheet with parchment.

Put the calamari in a medium bowl, sprinkle with the salt, black pepper, and cayenne, and toss thoroughly to coat.

Put the beaten eggs in a shallow bowl and the cassava flour in a second shallow bowl. Working in batches and using your left hand for the cassava flour and your right hand for the egg, put 3 or 4 calamari pieces into the egg mixture. Stick your right index finger into the center of the calamari tubes and spin them around to thoroughly coat the inside as well as outside with egg. Pick up the pieces and allow the excess egg to drip off, then put them in the flour and, using your dry hand, sprinkle the flour over the calamari to coat. Stick your left index finger in the center of the calamari tubes and spin them around to ensure they are completely coated inside and out. Shake off any excess flour and set the coated pieces aside on a plate. Repeat to coat the remaining calamari.

In a large sauté pan, melt ½ cup of the coconut oil over medium-high heat. When the oil is hot, working in batches, add the coated calamari to the pan and fry until golden and crispy, about 1 min-ute, then flip and fry on the second side for 1 minute. Use a slot-ted spoon to transfer the calamari to the prepared baking sheet and keep warm in the oven. Repeat until you have cooked half the calamari, then carefully discard the used cooking oil. Add the remaining ½ cup coconut oil to the pan, heat it over medium-high heat, and cook the remaining calamari (in batches, as needed). Serve with 999 island dressing.

1 pound calamari, cut into ½-inch rounds

1 teaspoon kosher salt

½ teaspoon freshly ground black pepper

½ teaspoon cayenne pepper

4 large eggs, beaten

2 cups cassava flour

1 cup coconut oil

999 Island Dressing (page 52)

celebration seafood pasta

Making delectable pasta is all about infusing the liquid you cook it in, and the secret to this dish is to cook the pasta in a luscious lobster stock made by parcooking the tails in their shells. Your grocer will have reasonably priced, smaller lobster tails. Roy makes this extraordinary special-occasion dish gluten-free for my birthday or to ring in the New Year. It is always filled with love, and good for the soul. What are you waiting for? SERVES 4 • COOK TIME: 2 HOURS

PREP THE LOBSTER: In a large stockpot, combine 3 quarts water and the salt and bring to a boil over high heat. Add the lobster tails and cook for 5 minutes. Remove the lobster tails with tongs, reserving the water in the pot, and set them aside to cool for 5 to 10 minutes. Skim any bubbly residue from the top and set the water aside to use in the stock.

Put a lobster tail on its side in a kitchen towel. Gently press down with both hands until you hear the shell crack. Flip the tail on its back and, using kitchen scissors, cut the shell right up the middle of the underside, being careful to only cut the shell and not the meat. Then, using the towel, gently pull the two halves of the shell apart. Carefully remove the meat from the shell, working slowly and deliberately in order to keep the meat in one piece. Some may be more difficult to pull out than others, and you may break some of the meat, which is fine—just do the best you can to keep them intact. Set the meat aside and reserve the shells for the stock.

FOR THE STOCK: In a large Dutch oven, heat the olive oil over medium heat. Add the celery, onion, salt, and pepper and stir to combine. Cook, stirring frequently, until the vegetables are

FOR THE LOBSTER

- 1 tablespoon kosher salt
- 5 small shell-on lobster tails (about 1 pound total) (about ¾ pound cooked—or more if feeling indulgent)

FOR THE LOBSTER STOCK

- ⅓ cup extra-virgin olive oil
- 1 cup very coarsely chopped celery (2-inch chunks)
- 1 cup very coarsely chopped yellow onion (1½-inch chunks)
- 1 teaspoon kosher salt
- 1 teaspoon freshly ground black pepper
- 5 garlic cloves, smashed and peeled
- 10 sprigs parsley

continued...

softened, about 6 minutes. Add the reserved lobster shells and cook, stirring frequently, until the vegetables are caramelized, about 5 minutes more.

Add the smashed garlic, the reserved lobster cooking water, and the parsley sprigs to the pot. Increase the heat to medium-high and bring the water to a boil, then immediately reduce the heat to low and cook at a bare simmer for 30 minutes.

Set a fine-mesh strainer over a large bowl. Use a slotted spoon to transfer the lobster shells and the vegetables from the stock into the strainer, capturing any drippings in the bowl. Discard the vegetables, then return any drippings in the bowl to the stockpot. Measure out ¾ cup stock and set aside for the sauce, and reserve the remaining stock in the stockpot for cooking the pasta.

FOR THE SAUCE: In a large saucepan, heat the olive oil over medium heat. Add the shallots and cook, stirring, until soft and translucent, about 2 minutes. Add the tomatoes, garlic, red pepper flakes, black pepper, and salt and stir to combine. Cover and cook for 5 minutes. Uncover and stir well. Cover and cook until the tomatoes start to break down, about 5 minutes more.

Add the wine and ¾ cup of the lobster stock, increase the heat, and cook until it starts to bubble again. Reduce the heat to medium-low and simmer, uncovered, stirring occasionally, to further break down the tomatoes and concentrate the sauce, about 20 minutes. Increase the heat to medium-high and add the butter. Cook, stirring, until the butter has melted. The sauce should now look honey-colored. Reduce the heat to medium-low and simmer, uncovered, for 5 minutes.

FOR THE SAUCE

- 3 tablespoons extra-virgin olive oil
- 1 cup chopped shallots
- 4 cups ripe pear tomatoes or cherry tomatoes
- 2 garlic cloves, minced
- 1 teaspoon red pepper flakes
- 1 teaspoon freshly ground black pepper
- ½ teaspoon kosher salt
- 1 cup dry white wine
- ½ cup (1 stick) unsalted butter, cut into pieces
- 1 pound large shrimp, peeled, tails left on, and deveined
- 1 pound bucatini pasta

  Chopped fresh flat-leaf parsley, for garnish (optional)

  Shredded Parmesan cheese, for garnish (optional)

TERI'S TIPS

This dish is best for 2 to 4 people. It would be hard to double.

While the sauce is cooking, bring the lobster stock back to a boil. Since there is not as much liquid to cook the pasta as you would normally use, you will need to hold the pasta upright in the pot until it begins to soften, then gradually press it down until it's completely submerged. (This takes a little patience, and works, but if there truly isn't enough stock to manage this, just add a cup or two of boiling water.) Cook the pasta, stirring occasionally, until al dente, about 8 minutes depending on the brand.

Meanwhile, cut the lobster tail meat in half lengthwise. Add the shrimp to the simmering tomato sauce and stir to combine. Cook for 2 minutes, then add the lobster meat and cook for 2 minutes more.

Drain the pasta (or remove it using tongs, as most of the stock will have been absorbed) and stir it into the sauce. Toss well to coat and cook for 1 to 2 minutes more to let the pasta absorb the sauce.

If desired, garnish with parsley and Parmesan cheese before serving.

family

Sharing my family recipes is an honor and a delight. These dishes have had their moments on my Instagram stories, and followers and fans have overwhelmingly requested the recipes, even though they are not necessarily Whole30. They are the dishes my kids grew up with, and for us they evoke family, home, love, and motherhood. Traditions are vital to human existence, and so many traditions take place when we gather around a table. The ritual of gathering for a meal cooked with love for loved ones creates the sweetest memories in the world. And that's what these recipes are for my family.

lucy's favorite potato pancakes

You just can't go wrong with these beauties. Although many friends serve them exclusively for holidays, I like to put a big platter in the middle of the kitchen table surrounded by three sauces—applesauce, sour cream, and ketchup—and call it dinner. By the way, if you make them a bit smaller and top them with salmon, sour cream, and chives, they become fantastic hors d'oeuvres. These are great served with Crisp Crunchy Cucumber Salad (page 238), Not Your Mother's Meat Loaf (page 252), or a simple green salad.

SERVES 6; MAKES 15 PANCAKES • COOK TIME: 45 MINUTES

I like to use both shredded and "dried," and finely processed potatoes to achieve the perfect crunchy, creamy pancakes. Using the shredding attachment on a food processor, shred all the potatoes. Put the shredded potatoes in a large bowl. Fit the food processor with the regular S-blade. Measure out 2 cups of the shredded potatoes and return that amount to the food processor. Pulse until the potatoes are finely chopped and set them aside.

Tip the shredded potatoes from the bowl into a dish towel and squeeze to remove as much liquid as possible, then return them to the bowl (or just use your hands to squeeze out excess liquid). Stir the finely chopped potatoes. Add the onion, flour, eggs, salt, and pepper to the bowl and stir to combine well. Set aside.

In a large skillet, heat the vegetable oil over high heat. Working in batches, scoop ¼ cup of the potato mixture per pancake into the hot oil and use a spoon to flatten each into a pancake shape; do not crowd the pan. Reduce the heat to medium and fry until crispy and golden brown on the bottom, about 2 minutes, then flip and fry for 2 minutes on the second side. If need be, raise the temperature to medium-high to keep the oil hot. Transfer the potato pancakes to a paper towel–lined plate. Repeat until done. Serve hot, with sour cream and applesauce, if desired.

4 pounds red potatoes, peeled

½ cup finely diced yellow onion

¼ cup all-purpose flour, or 3 tablespoons gluten-free all-purpose flour

2 large eggs, lightly beaten

2 teaspoons kosher salt

½ teaspoon freshly ground black pepper

1 cup vegetable oil

Sour cream or applesauce, for serving (optional)

"Family is anyone who loves you unconditionally." —Unknown

TERI'S TIPS
No food processor? Use the large holes on a box grater for the majority of the potatoes (the portion that you squeeze dry), and for the "finely processed" potatoes, just shred 2 cups using the smaller holes on the grater. Fry just one pancake to start (you'll probably ruin it anyway), as it will give you a better feel for the frying process.

minestrone

This soul-satisfying minestrone is so much fun to make for your family. Nothing makes me happier than loading a couple of bowls with all this goodness and watching my children devour it. There are many ways to change up this dish depending on what's local and in season. For example, add kale in the fall, potatoes and cabbage in the winter, and asparagus and green beans in the spring. If you're looking for a Whole30 version of something like this, make my Whole30 Vegetable Soup (page 84). SERVES 6 TO 8; MAKES 3 QUARTS

If using the bacon, in a medium stainless steel sauté pan, fry the bacon over medium heat until crispy, about 10 minutes. Remove the bacon from the pan and set aside. Discard all but 2 tablespoons of the fat from the pan.

Return the pan to medium heat and warm the bacon fat (if not using bacon fat, heat the olive oil or clarified butter instead). Add the carrots, onion, celery, and garlic and cook, stirring, for 3 minutes. Add the zucchini, squash, spinach, and basil and cook, stirring, for 1 minute more. Turn off the heat.

In a large stockpot, stir together the stock, 4 cups water, and the salt and bring to a boil over high heat. Add the penne and cook for 3 minutes. Add the potatoes and corn and cook until the pasta and potatoes are cooked through, about 7 minutes.

In a small bowl, combine the tomato paste with ¼ cup liquid from the stockpot and stir until mixed well and the paste has dissolved. Set aside.

Add the beans and peas to the stockpot.

5   slices bacon, cut into ½-inch squares (optional)

2   tablespoons olive oil or clarified butter (optional, if not using bacon)

1   cup chopped carrots

½   cup chopped yellow onion (¾-inch pieces)

½   cup chopped celery (¾-inch pieces)

2   tablespoons finely chopped garlic

1   cup chopped zucchini (¾-inch pieces)

1   cup chopped peeled yellow squash (¾-inch pieces)

1   cup coarsely chopped spinach

½   teaspoon dried basil

4   cups Chicken Stock (page 47)

1   tablespoon kosher salt

½   cup gluten-free penne pasta

1   cup sliced fingerling potatoes
    (1-inch pieces)

¾   cup frozen or fresh corn
    kernels

1   tablespoon tomato paste

¾   cup drained canned
    pinto beans

½   cup frozen peas

1   cup crushed tomatoes,
    pureed

3   cloves Garlic Confit (page 33),
    pressed

½   teaspoon freshly ground
    black pepper

½   teaspoon red pepper flakes
    (optional)

Add a little liquid from the pot to the vegetables in the sauté pan and heat over medium heat, gently scraping the bottom of the pan. Transfer the contents of the pan to the stockpot. Add the pureed tomatoes and the tomato paste mixture, the garlic confit, black pepper, and red pepper flakes (if using) and stir to combine well.

Serve garnished with the bacon, if desired.

TERI'S TIPS

I'm a bit of a lily-gilder and can't help myself, so feel free to skip the bacon and sauté the mirepoix in olive oil or clarified butter.

Barely cook (par-cook) the zucchini as it continues to cook in the soup.

"Grieve, so that you can be free to feel something else."
            —Nayyirah Waheed

thanksgiving

My favorite day of the year is Thanksgiving. I happen to have been born on Thanksgiving Eve—I arrived just in time to begin the cooking! Why is it my favorite holiday? It's a day about family, gratitude, and food, all of which live at the heart of this book.

I love the magic of a holiday. I love the anticipation and the planning, and it's worth all the hard work. I happily put my energy into preparing food with love, knowing my guests will taste that love in every bite. There is no clearer example of that concept than Thanksgiving dinner, a day when people are a little more kind, thankful, helpful and, at least in my family, end up feeling drunk on love!

As a lily-gilder, I like to take my parties a step further. Last Thanksgiving, I cleared my living room, borrowed a couple of tables, and lengthened my dining room table to three times its size. We created quite an extravaganza!

On a gorgeous summer night, I think nothing of dragging my lengthy kitchen table outside, chairs and all, for a real farm-to-table experience. If you have lovely crystal, silver, and fine china, bring it out. What are you waiting for? If you don't, bring out what you do have. Place settings don't need to match—a great mix-and-match look has always been my favorite. Transform your dinner party into an event! Your people will feel all the love and effort that make it spectacular. I grew up in a home that my mother filled with music, love, and laughter, though she wasn't crazy about cooking. For me, Thanksgiving—and quite frankly every day—is all about family, food, and love.

thanksgiving tips

1. Make a timeline for the two weeks before Thanksgiving, beginning with what time you plan to serve your dinner and going backward for two weeks. Include pulling all recipes together, ordering a turkey (and any other specialty items) and shopping for nonperishables a week ahead.
2. Look over your guest list and address any food allergies or restrictions, in case you need to add or modify a recipe.
3. Do yourself a favor and have every guest bring something. Choose wisely when you assign dishes—if you have a baker in the family, have them make a pie. People who prefer not to cook can pick up some drinks, as assigned by your beverage manager, or

pick up rolls from your favorite bakery. Be specific about what you'd like people to bring. The idea here is to eliminate surprises—that is the best way to help yourself succeed.

4. Décor! I love to use place cards. It's fun to decide where people are sitting, so that you have the chatty family members next to the quiet ones. Seat people in an unexpected place to create conversation. You can take a photo of everyone who is coming, put each into a small frame and incorporate it into the place setting, and have guests find where they are sitting. Another fun idea is to use baby pumpkins as a placeholder with a guest's name written on each of them. Small 5 × 5-inch cube vases stuffed with flowers are fun. Go to a discount store and see what inspires you. The sky is the limit!

5. Bring out your family heirlooms! If you have cherished family items, Thanksgiving is the time to use them. I bring out my mother's china and silver, my grandmother's gravy boat and dessert spoons—and it's fun to bring out something my kids made when they were little, too. This holiday is also about remembering those who are not with us. My symbol for my mother is a rooster, and I always have a special rooster decoration somewhere on the table.

6. Well in advance, pull out all your platters and utensils, label them for their intended uses (i.e., "turkey," "stuffing," etc). Take a photo of everything, return them all to their shelves/cupboards, and check that off your list.

7. Count the pieces you will be using (for example: 12 salad plates, 12 dinner plates, 12 forks, 12 knives, etc.) and leave a note at the top of the stack to show your tally and what they are. (Then after dinner, before the garbage is thrown out, make sure to count the pieces, especially the silverware, so you end up with what you started with; going on a treasure hunt through the garbage is never fun.)

8. The week before, wash the glasses and plates and polish your silver. If you are using cloth napkins and tablecloths, wash and iron them. Make sure you have what you need in advance, so you don't have to scramble at the last minute.

9. Consider what food prep you can do the days before. For example, if you are getting brave and making homemade stuffing, dry out your bread. Make turkey stock for stuffing a week in advance. I make my turkey drippings in advance. And if you've never made a turkey stock, it is a must-do that will absolutely change your holiday. Brine your turkey. I caramelize the onions 48 hours in advance for my onion soufflé. And the cranberry relish can be made a couple of days in advance. If you have never sugared nuts, this is the time to do it. Put all these food-prep steps (and more!) on your timeline.

10. Enlist help: assign each guest a job to do on the day of. In my house, we also rotate helping in the kitchen in two-hour shifts, with me at the helm. I make a timeline of who is helping at what time.

11. Figure out in advance who is doing the dishes. Consider hiring a college student for a couple of hours. I can assure you that I am never part of the crew doing the dishes after my Thanksgiving dinner—and you shouldn't be, either! You've been planning this event for two weeks, so relax and enjoy the fruits of your labor.

12. Assign larger jobs. For example, I designate a family member as a beverage manager who asks guests their drink preferences in advance, picks up everything needed, and sets up the bar the day of. That way, I don't have to wonder whether we have enough ice, or the right beverages for each person, and it also saves a lot of time and money, because instead of overbuying, you are purchasing only what your guests want to drink. Create your own signature drink! Pomegranate seeds are always nice at that time of year. Last year my niece, Alex, was in charge of drinks and created a festive cocktail that could also be made as a mocktail—we do like to go all out!

13. Be sure to take pictures of each dish to help plan for next year. Believe me, though we think we'll remember, it's a huge time-saver.

14. Take a breath, relax, and remember this holiday is all about gratitude.

15. Make a toast to your family members who are no longer here. If appropriate, you can share what you are grateful for. Be a guest at your own party.

16. If there is one day of the year to make special food, this is the day. It's all about making memories. Happy Thanksgiving!

crisp crunchy cucumber salad

You can't imagine how much people love this recipe. It seems so simple, but my cucumber salad is truly the best complement to everything from potatoes to grilled steak or fish. This creamy and crunchy home run is a regular in our refrigerator, and it will be in yours, too. SERVES 4 • COOK TIME: 10 MINUTES

In a medium bowl, combine the cucumbers, onion, dill, chives, vinegar, salt, and white pepper and stir gently to mix well. Let sit for 5 minutes.

In a small bowl, stir together the sour cream and maple syrup. Pour the mixture over the cucumbers and stir gently to combine. Serve.

- 4 cups cubed peeled seedless cucumbers (½- to 1-inch cubes)
- ½ cup finely chopped red onion
- ½ cup chopped fresh dill
- ½ cup chopped fresh chives
- 1 tablespoon plus 1 teaspoon white vinegar
- 1 teaspoon kosher salt
- ½ teaspoon ground white pepper
- ¾ cup sour cream
- 1 teaspoon real maple syrup (optional)

TERI'S TIPS

This dish is perfect to eat at the time you make it, but if you have leftovers, it's a great addition to your to-go lunch.

p.s.'s chili

This is one of Lucy's absolute favorites. I've adapted this recipe from my sister's kitchen. It's a great mild chili that your entire family will enjoy. I often double the recipe, as it's wonderful to freeze for another day! We like to top ours with poached eggs. SERVES 6 TO 8 • COOK TIME: 2½ HOURS

2 tablespoons extra-virgin olive oil

1 large yellow onion, chopped (about 1 cup)

1 garlic clove, pressed (about 1 teaspoon)

1½ pounds ground sirloin

1½ tablespoons chili powder

1 tablespoon kosher salt

1 bay leaf

1 teaspoon chipotle chile powder (optional)

1 teaspoon garlic salt

¼ teaspoon dried oregano

¼ teaspoon cayenne pepper

5 cups fire-roasted crushed tomatoes

1 cup high-quality jarred marinara sauce

2 (15-ounce) cans pinto, chili, or other beans, drained and rinsed

1 tablespoon balsamic vinegar

In a large Dutch oven, heat the olive oil over medium-high heat. Add the onion and garlic and cook, stirring, until translucent, about 5 minutes. Add the ground beef and cook, stirring and breaking up any lumps, until thoroughly cooked, about 10 minutes. Add the chili powder, salt, bay leaf, chipotle chile powder, if desired, garlic salt, oregano, and cayenne and cook, stirring, for 2 minutes.

In a food processor, working in batches if necessary, blend the tomatoes and marinara together. Add this mixture and the beans to the Dutch oven, then add 1 cup water and stir to combine well. Bring to a boil, then reduce the heat to medium-low and cook at a low simmer, uncovered, stirring occasionally, for 30 minutes. Reduce the heat to low, cover, and cook for 1½ hours more.

Stir in the vinegar, remove the bay leaf, and serve.

TERI'S TIPS

My family likes a mild version, so we leave out the chipotle chile powder. If you like it a little spicy, leave it in and serve with hot sauce.

My kids adore this with poached eggs and tortilla chips on top. It's also great in a stuffed baked potato with cheese on top.

"Come 'n' get it! It ain't getting any warmer!" —Lawrence Bell

lucy's egg salad
with whole30 variation

My daughter Lucy says, "This is the epitome of what coming home feels like," and let me tell you, it's certainly a very special recipe. The trick to making it delicate is to grate the eggs into tiny pieces and finely dice the other crunchy bits, creating a light and creamy treat infused with love. SERVES 4 • COOK TIME: 20 MINUTES

6   large eggs

1   tablespoon plus ¼ teaspoon kosher salt

½   cup high-quality mayonnaise, or Whole30 Mayonnaise (page 286), or more if desired

½   cup finely chopped celery

¼   cup finely chopped onion

¼   cup finely chopped fresh chives

½   teaspoon yellow mustard

¼   teaspoon freshly ground black pepper

Crisp Crunchy Cucumber Salad (page 238; optional)

TERI'S TIPS
Make extra for the next day.

Fill a medium pot with enough water to cover the eggs. Add 1 tablespoon of the salt. Bring the water to a boil. Add the eggs and cook for 8½ minutes. Remove the eggs from the pot and set aside to cool, about 10 minutes. When cool, crack and peel the eggs, discarding the shells. Using a box grater, grate the eggs into a large bowl.

Add the mayonnaise, celery, onion, chives, mustard, remaining ¼ teaspoon salt, and the pepper and stir until combined well. Serve alone or with cucumber salad, if desired.

"Until one becomes a mother, no one can ever tell you what it will feel like to love someone else so deeply and profoundly that you will rejoice when they rejoice, ache when they ache, feel what they feel—even without ever speaking a word."
—Jennifer Quinn

whole30 egg salad

Fill a medium pot with enough water to cover the eggs. Add 1 tablespoon of the salt. Bring the water to a boil. Add the eggs and cook for 8 minutes. Remove the eggs from the pot and set aside to cool, about 10 minutes. When cool, crack and peel the eggs, discarding the shells. Using a box grater, grate the eggs into a large bowl. Add the mayonnaise, celery, onion, chives, pepperoncini, mustard, remaining ½ teaspoon salt, and pepper to the eggs and stir until combined well. Serve.

6   large eggs

1   tablespoon plus ½ teaspoon kosher salt

½   cup Whole30 Mayonnaise (see page 286)

½   cup finely chopped celery

3   tablespoons finely chopped onion

3   tablespoons finely chopped fresh chives

¼   cup finely chopped jarred pepperoncini

½   teaspoon yellow mustard (check label for compliance if doing Whole30)

¼   teaspoon freshly ground black pepper

teri's epic salad
with wasabi-lime dressing

I'm a little bit famous in my circle of friends for this luncheon salad. Who doesn't search for the perfect salad—the right combination of greens, toppings, protein, and fabulous dressing? This is all that and more. One plate is simply not enough. I've been making this "celebration" salad for twenty-five years, and people are still talking about it. There's even a woman who hasn't had it in years, but still calls with hope in her voice, asking, "When are you making your Epic Salad next?" I'm not going to kid you—there are quite a few steps and it's a lot of work, but like its name says, it's EPIC! SERVES 8 • COOK TIME: 2 HOURS, PLUS AT LEAST 4 HOURS MARINATING TIME

FOR THE CHICKEN: In a blender, combine the olive oil, lime juice, vinegar, onion, garlic, oregano, salt, and pepper. Blend until smooth.

Put the chicken breasts in a shallow container, pour the marinade over, and toss well. Cover and refrigerate for at least 4 hours or up to overnight.

When ready to cook the chicken, preheat the oven to 350°F.

Remove the chicken from the refrigerator and let it come to room temperature. Arrange the chicken on a baking sheet and bake for 25 minutes (less time if you have smaller breasts). Remove from the oven and set aside.

In a large sauté pan, heat the olive oil over high heat. Once hot, reduce the heat to medium-high, add the chicken breasts, and sear until browned and cooked through, about 2 minutes per side. Remove from the pan and set aside. (If you prefer to grill the chicken, heat your grill to medium-high, then cook the chicken breasts for 5 minutes per side.) Once cool enough to handle, thinly slice the chicken across the grain and set aside.

FOR THE CHICKEN

- ½ cup extra-virgin olive oil
- ⅓ cup fresh lime juice
- ¼ cup red wine vinegar
- ¼ cup finely chopped yellow onion
- 1 tablespoon finely chopped garlic
- 1 teaspoon minced fresh oregano
- ½ teaspoon kosher salt
- ½ teaspoon freshly ground black pepper
- 4 skin-on boneless chicken breasts (see Tip)
- 1 tablespoon extra-virgin olive oil (for searing)

FOR THE TORTILLA STRIPS

- 24 fresh corn tortillas
- 4 cups vegetable oil
- Kosher salt

continued...

FOR THE TORTILLA STRIPS: Cut the tortillas into ¼-inch strips; to save time, stack 4 or 5 tortillas and cut them all at once.

In a large skillet, heat the vegetable oil over high heat until shimmering and reaches 350°F. Reduce the heat to medium, add 1 cup of the tortilla strips, and fry until crisp and golden, 1 to 2 minutes. Use a slotted spoon to transfer the tortilla strips to a paper towel–lined platter or baking sheet to drain and season with a sprinkle of salt. Repeat to fry the remaining strips, testing the oil temperature between the batches by frying one or two strips and increasing the heat if necessary.

ASSEMBLE THE SALAD: In a large bowl, begin to layer the salad ingredients, starting with the greens; sprinkle them lightly with salt. Add the carrots, olives, feta, scallions, half of the chicken, and one-third of the tortilla strips and toss to incorporate. Spoon ½ cup of the dressing over the mixture and toss again lightly to combine. Taste and dress accordingly.

Top with the remaining tortilla strips and the remaining chicken and serve.

FOR THE SALAD

About 16 cups lovely mixed lettuces (baby romaine, leaf, Boston, or a combination)

Kosher salt

2 cups finely julienned carrots (about 4 medium)

1½ cups pitted Kalamata olives (about 6 ounces), sliced in half

6 ounces feta cheese (sheep's milk, if possible), crumbled

¾ cup thinly sliced scallions

Wasabi-Lime Dressing (recipe follows)

TERI'S TIPS

Although it's a bit of work, parts of the salad can be done ahead. Make the dressing a day ahead. Marinate the chicken overnight, as it helps the chicken stay moist and juicy. The morning of, fry the tortilla strips and prep the vegetables.

A good rule of thumb for an entrée salad is two handfuls of lettuce per person.

Ideally, the chicken here is grilled—the grill imparts a great flavor. But if you don't have a grill (or if it's too cold outside), I love using this reverse-sear method, baking the chicken breasts gently in the oven first, then finishing them in a super-hot pan to get a golden, crispy crust.

wasabi-lime dressing

MAKES 2 CUPS • COOK TIME: 15 MINUTES

½ cup fresh orange juice
(from about 1 orange)

½ cup fresh Ruby Red grapefruit
juice (from about 1 grapefruit)

¼ cup plus 2 tablespoons fresh
lime juice (from about 3 limes)

¼ cup light sesame oil

1½ tablespoons wasabi powder

1 tablespoon pure maple syrup

1 tablespoon pressed garlic
(about 3 large cloves)

1½ teaspoons kosher salt

¼ teaspoon red curry paste

3 ounces soft fresh goat cheese

¼ cup coarsely chopped
fresh basil

¼ cup coarsely chopped
fresh cilantro

In a blender, combine the orange, grapefruit, and lime juices, the sesame oil, wasabi powder, and maple syrup and blend well. Add the garlic, salt, and red curry paste and blend to combine. Cut the goat cheese into small chunks and add them to the blender. Blend until smooth. Add the basil and cilantro and blend on low to finely chop and incorporate the herbs, but not completely macerate them.

plant-based chili

GLUTEN-FREE
DAIRY-FREE
GRAIN-FREE
(WITHOUT
TEMPEH)

Though I developed this recipe for my kids when they were little, it has remained a guest favorite in my kitchen. You don't have to be plant-based to love this chili. I recommend having a delicious vegan option up your sleeve, and this one is ideal. People are crazy about the combination of carrots, beets, lime, and black beans in this savory yet sweet chili. Sautéed tempeh croutons on top add a perfect crunch to each bite. Serve this with Patrick's Vegetarian Feast (page 269), and you have a plant-based dinner party.

SERVES 4 TO 6 • COOK TIME: 45 MINUTES

6	tablespoons extra-virgin olive oil
3½	cups cubed carrots (½-inch cubes)
1½	cups chopped yellow onions
1½	cups cubed red beets (½-inch cubes)
2	teaspoons kosher salt
¼	cup fresh lime juice
2	tablespoons coconut aminos
1	tablespoon pure maple syrup
2	teaspoons chili powder
1	teaspoon ground cumin
½	teaspoon red pepper flakes
1	(15-ounce) can organic black beans, drained and rinsed
1	(15-ounce) can organic kidney beans, drained and rinsed
⅓	cup chopped fresh cilantro
8	ounces tempeh, cut into 8 equal pieces

In a large pot, heat 3 tablespoons of the olive oil over high heat. Add the carrots, onions, beets, and salt and stir to combine. Cover, reduce the heat to medium-low, and cook for 10 minutes. Uncover and stir well. Cover and cook until the vegetables are tender, about 10 minutes more. Add the lime juice, coconut aminos, maple syrup, chili powder, cumin, and red pepper flakes and stir to combine well. Add ⅔ cup water, stir, and cook, uncovered, for 2 minutes. Add the black beans, kidney beans, and cilantro and stir to combine. Bring to a boil, then turn off the heat.

In a medium skillet, heat the remaining 3 tablespoons oil over medium-high heat. Reduce the heat to medium, add the tempeh, and cook evenly until golden brown on all sides, about 10 minutes total.

Serve the chili in bowls, topped with the tempeh.

patrick's chicken fingers

Your kids will certainly love these, but don't mistake them for a kids' dish, as the adults will be grabbing them, too. My love of these stems from a dish my dad used to make. In my house, they're a cause for celebration—dear friends often request them for dinner when they're arriving in town, and they make everything a bit better at the end of a tough day when a child needs to be cheered up. When you bite into one of these golden strips, you'll see why. It's a great idea to have a special family dinner once a week where you do something a little bit more. We always had Taco Tuesdays. These chicken fingers are also a great idea. Serve them with Not Your Mother's Meat Loaf (page 252). SERVES 4 • COOK TIME: 25 MINUTES

2 large boneless, skinless
   chicken breasts

1 teaspoon kosher salt

¼ teaspoon freshly ground
   black pepper

2 large eggs

2 tablespoons milk

1 cup all-purpose flour

1 cup vegetable oil

TERI'S TIPS

You can prep the chicken in the morning, lightly season it with salt and pepper, and put it in the fridge. And you can change these up by using fish rather than chicken.

Cut each chicken breast crosswise on an angle into 10 strips. Season the strips with the salt and pepper. Set aside.

Beat the eggs and milk together until the striations are gone, then pour them into a shallow, rimmed dish. Put the flour in a separate shallow, rimmed dish.

One by one, thoroughly cover each chicken strip in flour, then dredge in the egg, then remove and gently drop into the flour, covering thoroughly. Handling each chicken finger as minimally as possible, shake off any excess flour and set aside on a plate.

In a medium skillet, heat the vegetable oil over high heat until hot but not smoking (you can test the oil with a corner of a chicken strip—if it audibly sizzles, it's hot enough). Reduce the heat to medium-high. Working in batches, fry the chicken strips in the hot oil until golden brown, 2 to 3 minutes, flipping them halfway through. Transfer them to a tea towel–lined plate to drain. Repeat to cook the remaining chicken strips. Serve.

"When a child is learning how to walk and falls down fifty times, they never think to themselves, 'Maybe this isn't for me.'" —Unknown

not your mother's meat loaf
with sweet tomato glaze

This is a different spin on a sugary meat loaf because it's loaded with fresh herbs and easy to make gluten-free. The bacon helps seal in all the juices and imparts its smoky saltiness—so succulent. It's wonderful served with green beans and a Crisp Crunchy Cucumber Salad (page 238), and there is nothing better to take as a leftover to go the next day. SERVES 6 TO 8 • COOK TIME: 1¼ HOURS

Preheat the oven to 350°F.

FOR THE GLAZE: In a small bowl, stir together the ketchup, brown sugar, vinegar, and hot sauce until completely incorporated. Set aside (I always make double for dipping).

FOR THE MEAT LOAF: In a large bowl using your hands, mix together the beef, veal, pork, eggs, onion, bread crumbs, parsley, chives, basil, salt, and pepper. Form the mixture into an 8 × 6-inch loaf on a baking sheet. Cover the loaf with the bacon slices, laying them horizontally over the loaf, slightly overlapping, and tucking the ends underneath.

Bake for 45 minutes. Remove the meat loaf from the oven and brush on half the glaze. Return the pan to the oven and bake the meat loaf for about 15 minutes more, or until an instant-read thermometer inserted into the center reads 160°F. Remove from the oven, tent with foil, and allow to rest for 15 minutes before slicing and serving.

Serve with the remaining glaze on the side.

"Because I said so."—My mother

FOR THE GLAZE

- 1   cup ketchup
- ¼   cup brown sugar
- 3   tablespoons apple cider vinegar
- ½   teaspoon hot sauce

FOR THE MEAT LOAF

- 1   pound ground beef
- ½   pound ground veal
- ½   pound ground pork
- 2   large eggs
- 1   cup finely chopped yellow onion
- ¾   cup gluten-free white bread crumbs
- ¾   cup chopped fresh parsley
- ¼   cup chopped fresh chives
- 2   tablespoons chopped fresh basil
- 1½ teaspoons kosher salt
- ½   teaspoon freshly ground black pepper
- 8   slices bacon

TERI'S TIPS

 If you're avoiding sugar, this meat loaf is absolutely lovely without the glaze. As an alternative, serve it with Balsamic Tomato Confit (page 35).

bavarian pot roast

Here's a dish my mother made, shared by our dear friend Mary Torgerson. It reminds me of her, home, and family, and it's absolutely delicious—the beer and tomato sauce infused with the brown sugar becomes an exquisite sauce. I grew up having this pot roast with spaetzle, a kind of German dumpling. You can buy spaetzle dry, like pasta, and it's easy to prepare. But it's also great served with Creamy Leek Slaw (page 60), Old-School Red Cabbage with Bacon and Apples (page 281), and mashed potatoes.

SERVES 8 TO 10 • COOK TIME: UP TO 3 HOURS

Preheat the oven to 350°F.

In a Dutch oven, heat the olive oil over medium heat. Put the roast in the Dutch oven and brown it evenly on all sides, about 10 minutes total. Remove the roast from the pan and set aside. Discard the grease in the pot.

Return the roast to the Dutch oven, add the onion and bay leaf, and set aside.

In a food processor or blender, combine 1½ cups water, the crushed tomatoes, sugar, vinegar, cinnamon, salt, and ginger and process until thoroughly combined. Pour the mixture over the roast in the Dutch oven, then pour the beer over the roast.

Cover the Dutch oven and bake until the meat is cooked to your preferred doneness, 2 to 2½ hours. Remove the meat from the pot. Allow the meat to rest for 30 minutes. Carve the roast, then return the sliced meat to the sauce from the pot.

2 tablespoons extra-virgin olive oil or oil of your choice

1 (5-pound) rump roast

⅔ cup coarsely chopped onion

1 bay leaf

1 (8-ounce) can crushed tomatoes

2 tablespoons sugar

2 tablespoons red wine vinegar

1 tablespoon ground cinnamon

2 teaspoons kosher salt

1 teaspoon ground ginger

1 (12-ounce) bottle or can of ale or beer of your choice

"Be the generous side of fair."
—*Paula Turner*

caramelly poached pears

GLUTEN-FREE
DAIRY FREE
PALEO
GRAIN-FREE

My daughter, Lucy, was known for bringing these poached pears to school on her birthday—an unlikely massive success throughout her childhood, considering kids expect cake. All these years later, when I see those kids, they remember my poached pears. While we consider them a dessert, they pair perfectly with so many savory items, from pork chops to yogurt and granola. I make them in a big pan and let everyone dig in for the next few days. They absolutely melt in your mouth. SERVES 8 • COOK TIME: 30 MINUTES

1 cup unfiltered apple juice

½ teaspoon ground cinnamon

¼ teaspoon kosher salt

8 ripe but firm Bartlett pears, peeled, halved, and cored

In a medium bowl, combine ¼ cup water, the apple juice, cinnamon, and salt and stir well, until the cinnamon is thoroughly incorporated.

Arrange the pears cut side down in a single layer in a large skillet or wide pot with a lid. Put the pan on the stovetop. Evenly pour the apple juice mixture over the pears. Bring the liquid to a boil over high heat, then reduce the heat to medium, cover, and cook for 15 minutes.

Reduce the heat to medium-low, uncover, and simmer to reduce and thicken the sauce, about 10 minutes more. Serve pears with the liquid spooned over the top.

grandma post's egg rolls

We're bringing egg rolls back! Passed down from my grandma Post's recipe, the secret ingredient to these mouth-waterers is peanut butter. I grew up making them with my mom and have passed down this tradition to my kids, Patrick and Lucy. To celebrate each New Year, we used to fry them up, and my kids would enjoy being the delivery service, running them to our neighbors. Imagine how much my neighbors love me! MAKES ABOUT 18 ROLLS • COOK TIME: 1 HOUR

In a medium stainless steel sauté pan, melt 1½ tablespoons of the butter over medium heat. Add the celery, napa cabbage, shrimp, salt and pepper and cook, stirring, until the vegetables are barely cooked, about 2 minutes. Transfer the contents of the pan to a medium bowl. Add the chicken and scallions to the bowl, stir to combine well, then add the melted butter and stir to thoroughly coat. Stir in the peanut butter until well combined. Add the tamari and stir until well combined. Set aside.

Fill a large skillet one-quarter of the way up the side of the pan with vegetable oil and heat the oil over medium-high heat until it reaches 350°F.

Fill a small bowl with water and set it near you. Lay an egg roll wrapper down flat, with a corner pointing toward you, like a diamond. Dip your finger in the water and use it to moisten the wrapper along the edges. Put ⅓ cup of the filling in the center of the wrapper horizontally, then spread it out into a rectangle, leaving enough exposed wrapper on all edges to seal. Remoisten the edges with water, if needed, then fold the bottom corner up toward the center and, using a pulling-back motion, begin to slightly roll up to tighten up the mixture. Then fold the left and

1½	tablespoons unsalted butter, plus ⅓ cup unsalted butter, melted
2	cups finely chopped celery
2	cups thinly sliced napa cabbage
2	cups coarsely chopped cooked shrimp (about ¾ pound)
1	teaspoon kosher salt
½	teaspoon freshly ground black pepper
3	cups coarsely chopped cooked chicken breasts (we use poached)
1	cup sliced scallions
⅓	cup creamy peanut butter
1½	tablespoons tamari or soy sauce
	Vegetable or peanut oil, for frying
18	egg roll wrappers
	Sweet-and-sour sauce, for serving
	Spicy Almond Sauce (page 63), for serving

continued...

right corners in toward the center and continue rolling up like a burrito. Repeat with the remaining egg roll wrappers and filling.

One at a time, gently place the egg rolls in the hot oil and, watching closely, fry until golden brown, 1 to 1½ minutes, flipping halfway through. Use a slotted spoon to transfer them to a paper towel–lined plate.

Serve with sweet-and-sour sauce and spicy almond sauce for dipping.

TERI'S TIPS

Don't open the egg roll wrapper package until you are ready to roll. If they are out in the air, they will dry out.

Only fry up what you need.

"Good-byes are only for those who love with their eyes. Because for those who love with heart and soul there is no such thing as separation."—Rumi

monie's carrot cake

This family favorite is something my dear friend Monie made for many of our get-togethers. When she moved to London, the torch was passed to me. I love to cook, but I am a reluctant baker. However, everybody needs a couple of desserts in their repertoire, and this is one of mine. It's absolutely delicious—and by the way, it's the breakfast of champions. **SERVES 12 • COOK TIME: 1 HOUR**

2	cups sugar
1½	cups vegetable oil, plus more for greasing
4	large eggs
2	cups all-purpose flour, plus more for dusting
2	teaspoons baking soda
2	teaspoons ground cinnamon
½	teaspoon freshly grated nutmeg
3	cups grated carrots
½	cup chopped pecans
¼	cup dark raisins
	Cream Cheese Frosting (recipe follows)

"Never ask a woman who is eating out of a pint of ice cream how she's doing." —Unknown

Preheat the oven to 350°F. Grease two 9- or 10-inch round cake pans, then line the bottoms with parchment paper cut to fit and grease the paper. Dust both pans with flour, tapping out any excess.

In a large bowl using a handheld mixer (or a whisk, if you're in the mood) or in the bowl of a stand mixer fitted with the whisk attachment, mix together the sugar and oil. One at a time, add the eggs, beating until well combined.

In a separate bowl, sift together the flour, baking soda, cinnamon, and nutmeg. Gradually add the sifted dry ingredients to the egg mixture and mix until smooth. Add the carrots, nuts, and raisins and stir by hand until incorporated. Set aside.

Divide the batter evenly into between the prepared pans. Bake for 30 to 35 minutes. Start checking at 25 minutes. You know it's done when a toothpick stuck into the middle comes out clean, with no batter. Remove from the oven and let cool completely. Run a knife around the edge of the cake pans and unmold the cakes, discarding the parchment. Frost in layer-cake fashion with the cream cheese frosting.

cream cheese frosting

MAKES ABOUT 4¾ CUPS

½ cup (1 stick) unsalted butter, at room temperature

1 (8-ounce) package cream cheese, at room temperature

1 pound confectioners' sugar, sifted

3 tablespoons fresh lemon juice

2 teaspoons vanilla extract

In a large bowl using a handheld mixer or in the bowl of a stand mixer fitted with the whisk attachment, cream the butter and cream cheese together. Add the sugar, lemon juice, and vanilla and beat thoroughly until completely creamy and smooth.

TERI'S TIPS

You want your frosting firm enough to spread. Sometimes the frosting needs a bit of tightening up—feel free to add 2 to 4 tablespoons more confectioners' sugar if the frosting seems too runny.

vegetables and side dishes

Vegetables are where it's at! I am a vegetable-forward cook, living for the farmers' market and eating seasonally. Nothing makes me feel more truly alive than waking at dawn to greet a bustling market as it opens, talking to the farmers, touching the vegetables, and seeing what's in season. Farmers' markets are the heartbeat of the community, and I feel the same kind of love for them as I do for bakers and sausage makers. Occasionally, I prefer to go to the farmers' market alone, so my family and friends don't rush me or ask me when we're leaving. It's such a soulful experience. It's taught me in the truest sense how to live in the moment and savor every ounce of life both inside and outside the market. While I am by no means a vegetarian, I'm always delighted by how many vegan and vegetarian followers I have, including my own son, who himself is a fantastic raw vegan cook and vegetable lover. They understand that my techniques translate into tips they can use.

zucchini ribbons with ginger marinade

Hooray for summer! When zucchini is in season, we embrace it, eating it for breakfast, lunch, and dinner. Topping it off with the refreshing ginger marinade is a great way to eat lightly and deliciously in the summer. This is simplicity at its best. SERVES 4 • COOK TIME: 15 MINUTES

Season the zucchini planks with ⅛ teaspoon of the salt and the pepper.

In a large sauté pan or grill pan, heat 1 teaspoon of the olive oil over high heat. When the oil is hot, reduce the heat to medium and spread the zucchini planks in the pan in a single layer (work in batches if they don't all fit at the same time). Cook until the zucchini is fork-tender but not mushy, about 1½ minutes per side.

In a bowl, stir together the remaining 2 tablespoons olive oil, the lime juice, scallions, garlic, ginger juice, and remaining ¼ teaspoon salt.

Pour the marinade over the zucchini. Serve.

2   medium zucchini, sliced lengthwise into about 6 (¼-inch-thick) planks each

⅛   teaspoon plus ¼ teaspoon kosher salt

¼   teaspoon freshly ground black pepper

2   tablespoons plus 1 teaspoon extra-virgin olive oil

2   tablespoons fresh lime juice

2   tablespoons chopped scallions

1   tablespoon pressed garlic

Juice from 1 tablespoon grated fresh ginger (see page 296)

green beans almondine

Here's my fresh take on an absolute classic. I've updated this old standby with a more healthful profile. There's nothing like the subtle flavor of crispy green beans quickly sautéed and then mixed with slivered and just-toasted almonds. Done correctly, these can be as irresistible as a french fry. SERVES 4 • COOK TIME: 15 MINUTES

Fill a large pot with water, add 1 tablespoon of the salt, and bring to a boil over high heat. Prepare a large bowl of ice water.

Add the green beans to the boiling water and cook for 3 minutes. Drain and plunge into the ice water; let cool for 5 minutes. Drain again and dry the beans. Set aside.

In a medium sauté pan, heat the olive oil over medium-high heat. Add the almonds and cook, stirring, until golden, 1 to 2 minutes.

Increase the heat to high, add the green beans, garlic, ¼ teaspoon salt, and the pepper, and stir to combine well. Cook, stirring, until the garlic is golden and the green beans are tender, about 2 minutes more.

Serve.

- 1 tablespoon plus ¼ teaspoon kosher salt
- 1 pound French green beans
- 1 tablespoon extra-virgin olive oil
- 3 tablespoons slivered almonds
- 6 garlic cloves, thinly sliced (about 4 tablespoons)
- ¼ teaspoon freshly ground black pepper

"Without rain, nothing grows; learn to embrace the storms in your life."   —*Unknown*

carrots with fennel

Fennel and carrots are a match made in heaven. This delightful pair combine to make a dish that is the perfect amount of crunchy and sweet. It feels updated and new, and is beautiful on the dinner table.

SERVES 4 • COOK TIME: 25 MINUTES

3 tablespoons clarified butter

1 cup thinly sliced fennel

½ cup chopped shallots

4 large carrots, cut on the bias into ¼-inch-thick slices (4 cups)

1 teaspoon kosher salt

"Food for us comes from our relatives, whether they have wings or fins or roots. That is how we consider food. Food has a culture. It has a history. It has a story. It has relationships."
—*Winona LaDuke*

In a large sauté pan, melt 2 tablespoons of the clarified butter over medium heat. Add the fennel and shallots and cook, stirring continuously, until soft and lightly golden, about 8 minutes. Using a slotted spoon, transfer the shallots and fennel to a bowl and set aside.

Add the remaining 1 tablespoon clarified butter to butter remaining in the pan and melt over medium heat. Add the carrots and cook, stirring, until the soft, about 9 minutes. Add the salt and stir to combine. Return the fennel and shallots to the pan and stir together. Serve.

TERI'S TIPS

The mushrooms are the entrée, so leave them whole
or slice them into large, beautiful pieces.

This dish is all about lightly cooking the vegetables, al dente, so even days later they
look amazing as part of a last-minute dinner, a to-go lunch, or a frittata. You will
have properly cooked vegetables that go with absolutely everything.

patrick's vegetarian feast
with cashew crema

Pull out your biggest sauté pan and get ready for a flavorful and hearty feast. A perfect entrée, this is ready in no time and can be changed up with your seasonal favorites. It packs a delicious punch! Serve it on a large platter with Cashew Crema and Gomasio, and watch everyone dig in. If you're lucky enough to have leftovers, top with an egg for a fantastic breakfast the next day. SERVES 4 • COOK TIME: 15 MINUTES

7½   tablespoons extra-virgin olive oil

16   ounces shiitake or other exotic mushrooms

2½   teaspoons kosher salt

1   cup chopped yellow bell peppers

12   ounces sugar snap peas (about 4 cups), blanched for 3 minutes then sliced on the diagonal into 3 pieces each (see page 296)

12   ounces Broccolini, florets gently separated and stems sliced ¼ inch thick (about 3 cups)

6   garlic cloves, chopped (about 4 tablespoons)

5   ounces kale leaves, sliced on an angle into ¼-inch-wide strips (about 4 cups)

Marinated Red Onions (page 30)

Gomasio (page 36)

Cashew Crema (page 65)

In a large nonstick pan, heat 2 tablespoons of the olive oil over medium-high heat. Add half the mushrooms and cook for 4 minutes, flipping halfway through. Add ½ teaspoon of the salt, stir to combine, cover, and cook for 1 minute. Uncover and cook until the mushrooms are cooked thoroughly but not overcooked, about 2 minutes more. Transfer the mushrooms to a bowl and set aside. Repeat with the remaining mushrooms.

In the same pan, heat 1 tablespoon of the olive oil. Add the peppers, sugar snap peas, and a pinch of salt and stir together. Cook, stirring continuously, for 2½ minutes. Transfer to a bowl and set aside.

In the same pan, heat 1½ tablespoons of the olive oil. Add the Broccolini and cook, stirring continuously, for 1½ minutes. Add half the chopped garlic and a pinch of salt and cook, stirring continuously, for 1½ minutes. Set aside.

In the same pan, heat the remaining 1 tablespoon olive oil over high heat. Add the kale, the remaining garlic, and a pinch of salt and cook, stirring continuously, until the kale is crispy, about 2½ minutes.

On a large platter, build your feast by arranging each vegetable in groups. Top with marinated onions and gomasio. Serve with cashew crema alongside.

sweet potato crostini
topped with mushrooms and cashew crema

This impromptu creation was inspired by a bountiful trip to my local farmers' market. Sweet potato crostini made a spectacular bed for the assorted mushrooms. When I added a dollop of Cashew Crema, a star was born! This wonderful play on a gluten-free Whole30 appetizer does not leave you feeling one bit deprived. If you can find them, the drier Japanese sweet potatoes make all the difference, especially if you think you don't like sweet potatoes. This is the perfect technique for making sweet potato rounds, so if you've never done it, don't hesitate! Part of the trick is to cut the sweet potatoes to the right thickness to get them perfectly crispy. Ideally, the mushrooms are crispy, too, and the textures will be a perfect marriage. Although you can do each element an hour ahead, don't assemble the dish until you are ready to eat. Great served with a salad and a grilled skirt steak for dinner. SERVES 6; MAKES ABOUT 40 CROSTINI • COOK TIME: 45 MINUTES

FOR THE SWEET POTATO CROSTINI

- 4½ teaspoons extra-virgin olive oil
- 2 or 3 medium Japanese sweet potatoes, cut into 40 (¼-inch-thick) rounds (see Tip)
- ¾ teaspoon kosher salt

FOR THE MUSHROOMS

- 3 tablespoons clarified butter
- 4 cups sliced mixed mushrooms (11 or 12 ounces)
- ⅛ teaspoon kosher salt
- ⅛ teaspoon freshly ground black pepper
- ¼ cup finely chopped shallots

FOR THE CROSTINI: Preheat the oven to 400°F. Line two large baking sheets with parchment paper. Using a pastry brush, brush the parchment with 2¼ teaspoons of the olive oil.

Arrange the sweet potato rounds on the prepared baking sheets in a single layer. Using the pastry brush, swipe the tops of the sweet potatoes with the remaining 2¼ teaspoons olive oil. Season the potatoes with the salt. Bake for 11 to 15 minutes, until the potatoes are beginning to crisp up, then flip them using a small spatula and bake for 11 to 15 minutes more, until golden brown. Remove from the oven and set the crostini aside to cool.

FOR THE MUSHROOMS: In a large skillet, heat 2 tablespoons of the clarified butter over medium-high heat until sizzling. Add the mushrooms and cook, stirring continuously, until crisp (not soggy!), 7 to 9 minutes, increasing the heat to high for the last minute of cooking. Once the liquid from the mushrooms has

continued...

completely cooked off, season with the salt and pepper. Transfer the mushrooms to a medium bowl and set aside.

In the same pan, melt the remaining 1 tablespoon clarified butter over medium heat. Add the shallots and cook, stirring, until translucent, 1 to 2 minutes. Add the garlic and cook, stirring continuously, until the garlic releases its aroma, about 30 seconds. Be sure to watch carefully, as garlic burns easily. Transfer the contents of the pan to the bowl with the mushrooms and stir gently to combine.

Spoon some of the mushroom-shallot mixture over each of the potato crostini. Finish by topping each with a small dollop of cashew crema and a sprinkle of chives. Serve.

2 teaspoons finely chopped garlic

Cashew Crema (page 65)

2 tablespoons finely chopped fresh chives

TERI'S TIPS

Cooking sweet potatoes can be tricky. Depending on your oven, the size of the potatoes, and the placement of the oven rack, the cooking time might vary. I can do one batch that takes 11 minutes per side, and another batch that takes 15 minutes per side. My advice: Watch them carefully, flip when necessary, and remove individual pieces as they are done.

gluten-free summer corn and zucchini fritters

These are crispy and light on the outside, yet delicately moist on the inside. People go absolutely crazy for them, so they are often gobbled up before they leave the flame. Crunchy yet creamy, these pair perfectly with just about any dish; you simply cannot make too many. SERVES 4 TO 6; MAKES 15 FRITTERS • COOK TIME: 35 MINUTES

In a large bowl, combine the corn, zucchini, 1 cup of the flour, the leek, salt, and pepper. Add the coconut milk and egg and mix until thoroughly combined. Set aside.

In a large sauté pan, melt 3 tablespoons of the coconut oil over medium heat. Fry a test fritter: Measure a scant ¼ cup of the fritter mixture into the pan and use a spoon to gently flatten it just a bit. Fry the fritter, flipping it to the other side when it starts to brown, for 6 to 7 minutes. If you find the mixture is too loose, add the remaining ¼ cup flour to the fritter mixture before continuing. Working in batches, fry the fritters, transferring them to a paper towel–lined plate to drain as they're done and adding another tablespoon of coconut oil to the pan between batches as needed. If the fritters brown too fast, reduce the heat to medium-low. If there are burned bits in the oil between batches, be sure to scoop them out before starting a new batch.

Serve with smoky red pepper sauce.

"A woman is like a tea bag—you can't tell how strong she is until you put her in hot water."
—Eleanor Roosevelt

2	cups fresh corn kernels (from about 2 large ears, or use frozen)
1	cup grated zucchini
1 to 1¼	cups Bob's Red Mill all-purpose gluten-free flour, or 1¼ cups regular all-purpose flour
¾	cup diced leek (white and pale green parts only)
1½	teaspoons kosher salt
½	teaspoon freshly ground black pepper
¾	cup full-fat unsweetened coconut milk, blended
1	large egg, lightly beaten
3 to 4	tablespoons coconut oil
	Smoky Red Pepper Sauce (page 62)

TERI'S TIPS

This eats lovely as a week-night dinner with a salad.

tangy stuffed baked potatoes

Who doesn't love a baked potato? It stands to reason that if a baked potato is good, a twice-baked potato would be twice as good! With very little preparation, this is a fabulous side dish, or an easy all-in-one meal on a weeknight. Sausage, Roasted Red Pepper Sauce, and my famous Marinated Red Onions make this the type of thing you'll want to eat every single day. SERVES 4 • COOK TIME: 1¾ HOURS

4 large russet potatoes

1½ teaspoons extra-virgin olive oil

2 teaspoons kosher salt

12 ounces precooked sausages, your choice of flavor (check label for compliance if doing Whole30), quartered lengthwise and diced

¼ cup clarified butter

Smoky Red Pepper Sauce (page 62)

Marinated Red Onions (page 30)

TERI'S TIPS

You can do the potatoes ahead and refrigerate overnight. Reheat them in the oven the next day while cooking the sausages.

Preheat the oven to 375°F.

Wash and dry the potatoes. Coat them with ½ teaspoon of the olive oil, then sprinkle with 1 teaspoon of the salt. Using a fork, poke the top of each potato twice and the bottom twice. Put them on a baking sheet and bake for 1 to 1½ hours, until cooked through. Remove from the oven and let cool for 10 minutes.

In a large sauté pan, heat the remaining 1 teaspoon olive oil over medium-high heat. Add the sausages and cook, stirring, until browned and crispy, about 5 minutes. Remove from the heat and set aside.

Once the potatoes are cool, slice off and discard the top quarter of each potato. Carefully scoop the flesh of the potatoes into a medium bowl, leaving the skin intact like a shell. Add the clarified butter and the remaining 1 teaspoon salt to the bowl with the scooped-out potatoes and stir to combine well. Spoon the potato mixture into the potato skins.

Top each potato with the cooked sausages, 2 tablespoons of the smoky red pepper sauce and a generous amount of marinated onions. Serve.

"I explain my 'hustle' very simply: I'm willing to do what most people 'won't' for much longer than they think they 'can't.'"

—*Myleik Teele*

old-school red cabbage, apples, and bacon

GLUTEN-FREE
DAIRY-FREE
WHOLE30
PALEO
GRAIN-FREE

A perfect balance of sweet, salty, and crunchy: the sautéed apples, thinly sliced crunchy red cabbage, and delicious salty bites of bacon are a lovely mix of flavors and textures. And who doesn't love an extra sprinkle of bacon on top? Pair this with my Bone-In Pork Schnitzel (page 171) and Creamy Leek Slaw (page 60), and you have a winner. SERVES 4 • COOK TIME: 20 MINUTES

8   ounces sliced bacon (check label for compliance if doing Whole30)

5   cups thinly sliced red cabbage (about ⅔ of a small head)

1   cup peeled and thinly sliced apple

1   tablespoon white vinegar

1   teaspoon kosher salt

¼   teaspoon freshly ground black pepper

Bring a large pot of water (about 4 quarts) to a boil over high heat.

Meanwhile, in a large skillet over medium-high heat, fry the bacon until done, 6 to 8 minutes. Transfer the bacon to a cutting board, leaving as much bacon fat in the pan as possible, and slice into ½-inch pieces. Set aside.

Pour the bacon fat into a bowl. Measure 2 tablespoons of the bacon fat, return it to the pan, and discard the remaining fat. Set the pan aside.

Add the red cabbage to the boiling water and cook until tender but still a bit crunchy, about 3 minutes. Drain the cabbage and set aside.

Heat the reserved bacon fat over medium-high heat. Add the apple and cook, stirring, until just soft, about 1 minute. Add the cabbage, bacon, vinegar, salt, and pepper and stir to combine thoroughly. Serve.

everyday greens

I'm a gal who loves greens 365 days a year. My philosophy is, a day well spent is one in which you eat greens as part of at least one meal, preferably breakfast. I like to cook them hot with salt and golden garlic. There are so many greens to choose between. For thick-stemmed greens like kale, I like to pull the leaves off the stems and freeze the stems to use when I make vegetable stock. Greens fill me with life force and vitality. SERVES 2 • COOK TIME: 5 MINUTES

In a medium sauté pan, heat 1 tablespoon of the olive oil over medium heat. Add the garlic and cook, stirring continuously, until it begins to turn brown, making sure not to burn the garlic, about 45 seconds. Immediately remove the garlic and set aside. Increase the heat to medium-high and add the remaining 1 tablespoon olive oil to the pan. Add the greens and ½ teaspoon salt and cook, stirring continuously, until the greens have wilted to your liking, 1½ to 2 minutes. Serve.

2 tablespoons extra-virgin olive oil

5 garlic cloves, chopped or sliced

1 pound kale, stemmed, leaves cut crosswise into ½-inch-wide slices

½ teaspoon kosher salt

"When you're green, you are growing." —Ray Kroc

> ### TERI'S TIPS
> It's important to have greens at every meal; not only are they delicious, but you feel so good after eating them. Buy them fresh weekly. Head to your local farmers' market as often as possible, and along the way discover a whole lot of vegetables that you knew nothing about.

building blocks

Learning to make these essential building blocks for Whole30 recipes is a great way to improve your skills in the kitchen. Transforming eggs and oil into a Whole30 mayo is the jumping-off point to a great sauce, and it's a key ingredient to a successful Whole30. You will use it in coleslaw, tuna salad, chicken salad, dressings, and sauces. You can puree roasted pepper or preserved lemon into it. You may use it as the base for your own unique mayo-based Magic Elixirs. Perfect Oven Bacon is a game-changer because it's less messy and more consistent. Blanching and parcooking are necessities to preserve the taste, texture, and color of vegetables. You'll find these, and all my building blocks and basics, life-changing.

whole30 mayonnaise

When someone says to me, "I'm prepping for a Whole30," I tell them the first thing to do is make a Whole30 mayonnaise, because it will be the base for so many Magic Elixirs, including Green Goddess (page 54), tartar sauce, and coleslaw. While I am a proponent of regular olive oil, for this recipe, light olive oil is an absolute must. Once you have a Whole30 mayonnaise, let your imagination guide you. Blend a roasted red pepper into Whole30 mayo for a specialty sauce. Add Garlic Confit (page 33) for a garlic mayo, or blend in Tomato Confit (page 35) for a smoky tomato flavor. Stir in diced olives and chopped tarragon for the loveliest fish sauce ever. Amp up this foundational ingredient in your own unique way—you can even bake it on top of salmon. Add Preserved Meyer Lemons (page 38) or avocado. The list is almost endless. MAKES 2 CUPS • COOK TIME: 5 MINUTES

Put the egg in a large mason jar and, using an immersion blender, blend the egg with ¼ cup of olive oil, pumping gently with a circular up-and-down motion. Add remaining oil in a thin stream until emulsified. Add the dry mustard, salt, and pepper and blend until combined. Add the lemon juice and blend to mix well. Put the lid on the jar and store in the refrigerator for up to 6 days.

1½   cups light olive oil
2   large eggs
½   teaspoon dry mustard
¼   teaspoon kosher salt
¼   teaspoon freshly ground black pepper
     Juice from 1 lemon

"The most important skill is simply showing up every day for a long time." —James Altucher

TERI'S TIPS

Occasionally the mayo will not emulsify. If that happens, crack an egg in another mason jar, put the immersion blender in the jar, start to blend slowly while adding the broken mayo, lifting up to the top and down in a circular motion.

TERI'S TIPS

I use an immersion blender, but if you have a small food processor with a little hole in the top of the lid, you can use that to slowly add the oil.

Be sure to label the jar with the date.

whole sisters' ranch

Whole Sisters' ranch dressing is one of the few recipes in this book that isn't my own—which should tell you something about how wonderful it is. The Whole Sisters are two real-life sisters specializing in healthful, clean food, and their dressing is a staple in my kitchen. MAKES 1⅔ CUPS • COOK TIME: 10 MINUTES

1   cup light olive oil

½   cup full-fat unsweetened coconut milk, blended

1   large egg

2   tablespoons red wine vinegar

1   tablespoon fresh lemon juice

1   teaspoon kosher salt

1   teaspoon freshly ground black pepper

¾   teaspoon onion powder

¾   teaspoon granulated garlic

3   tablespoons chopped fresh parsley

In a wide-mouth mason jar, combine the olive oil, coconut milk, egg, vinegar, lemon juice, salt, black pepper, onion powder, and granulated garlic and blend with an immersion blender for about 1 minute, until completely emulsified. Incorporate the parsley in the last 15 seconds (or it will turn your ranch green). Use immediately or seal the jar and store in the fridge up to 1 week, if you still have any left!

sweet potato crisps

This bit of heaven is not meant to be a main course, but you'll probably want it to be. A magnificent Whole30 addition, this can be a "food with no brakes," so proceed with caution. Use these as a breakfast highlight with eggs, tuck them into a salad, or offer them as a crisp with roast beef—however you serve them, they are simply sublime. Using coconut oil keeps the potatoes very crispy. Absolutely use Japanese sweet potatoes with drier, yellow flesh. SERVES 4 • COOK TIME: 15 MINUTES

In a large skillet, melt the coconut oil over high heat. When the oil is hot, reduce the heat to medium-high and, working in about three batches, add the sweet potato slices and fry until golden, 1 to 2 minutes, flipping them halfway through. Using a slotted spoon, transfer the sweet potato crisps to a paper towel–lined plate to drain. Sprinkle with kosher salt. Repeat to cook the remaining slices, layering them on the plate and seasoning with salt as you go.

1 cup coconut oil

2 Japanese sweet potatoes, sliced super thin (a mandoline helps)

Kosher salt

"But one of the things I have learned during the time I have spent in the United States is an old African-American saying: 'Each one, teach one.' I want to believe that I am here to teach one and, more, that there is one here who is meant to teach me. And if we each one teach one, we will make a difference."
—Marcus Samuelsson

potato croutons

I love the idea of using potato as a crouton. It's a great little addition or side dish, or a snack to go. Pair the croutons with a roasted chicken breast and a smear of Pistachio Pesto (page 51). Mix it up and add chili powder, smoked paprika, or red pepper flakes. These are what we'd call a "food with no brakes" in Whole30 language—you can't just eat one. So tuck in a few here and there, use them sparingly, and hide them from yourself if you need to. SERVES 4 • COOK TIME: 1 HOUR

1	tablespoon plus ½ teaspoon kosher salt
1½	pounds fingerling potatoes
2	tablespoons plus 1 teaspoon of extra-virgin olive oil
1	teaspoon chopped fresh rosemary
1	teaspoon chopped fresh thyme
½	teaspoon freshly ground black pepper

TERI'S TIPS
You can use medium Yukon Gold potatoes, but boil them for 15 minutes instead of 10.

Preheat the oven to 400°F.

Fill a medium pot with 2 quarts water, add 1 tablespoon of the salt, and bring to a boil over high heat. Add the potatoes and cook for 10 minutes. Drain and let cool, then cut the potatoes into cubes about the size of croutons.

In a medium bowl, stir together the olive oil, rosemary, thyme, remaining ½ teaspoon salt, and the pepper. Add the potatoes and toss to coat evenly. Transfer to a baking sheet. Roast for 15 minutes, or until beginning to brown. Remove from the oven, flip the potatoes over, and roast for 15 minutes more, or until well browned and crisped.

sweet potato croutons

MAKES 2 CUPS • COOK TIME: 35 MINUTES

Preheat the oven to 375°F. Line a baking sheet with parchment paper.

In a medium bowl, combine the sweet potato cubes, olive oil, salt, and pepper and toss until thoroughly coated. Spread them out on the prepared baking sheet and bake for 30 minutes, flipping halfway through, until cooked through and crispy. Transfer to a platter for serving.

"I believe that every child in this world needs to have a relationship with the land . . . to know how to nourish themselves . . . and to know how to connect with the community around them."
—Alice Waters

2 cups cubed peeled sweet potatoes (½-inch cubes)

1 tablespoon extra-virgin olive oil

½ teaspoon kosher salt

¼ teaspoon freshly ground black pepper

TERI'S TIPS

Sweet potatoes vary in moisture and sugars and can be finicky when you cook them, so be sure to watch them carefully to make sure they don't burn. Some can take 20 minutes, and some can take 35 minutes. Watch it!

jammy eggs

GLUTEN-FREE
DAIRY-FREE
WHOLE30
PALEO
GRAIN-FREE

A "jammy egg" is an egg somewhere between soft-boiled and hard-boiled. They're a delight; the white of the egg looks like hard-boiled, but the yolk has almost the consistency of jam and the color is a beautiful golden yellow. It's ideal for salads and for breakfast. It's far more delicious that a hard-boiled egg and adds true richness to any dish. The cooking time will vary depending on your pan or stove; my perfect egg is 7½ minutes, but once you figure out the perfect timing for yours, jot it down here in the book so that you'll know for the next time. **MAKES 6 SERVES 3 TO 6 • COOK TIME: 15 MINUTES**

1   tablespoon kosher salt

6   large eggs

"It's quite possible things will turn out far better than you can imagine." —Unknown

Fill a medium saucepan with 2 quarts water, add the salt, and bring to a gentle boil over medium-high heat. Prepare a large bowl of ice water.

Carefully add the eggs to the boiling water and cook for 7½ minutes, adjusting the heat as necessary to prevent the water from boiling too rapidly and cracking the eggs. Immediately remove them from the water with a slotted spoon and gently transfer them to the bowl of the ice water. Let them rest for 1 minute.

Transfer the eggs to a cutting board. They will continue to cook in the shells, so work quickly. With the end of a butter knife, gently crack the shells, immediately peel the eggs, and cut each in half. Serve.

perfect oven bacon

Oven bacon is a revelation. It's less mess and much easier. Try it once, and you'll never cook bacon on the stovetop again. As much as I would love to give you the exact recipe, I can only provide a framework, because there are a few variables, including how hot your oven runs, the weight of your baking sheet, and the thickness and type of your bacon, so use this as a guideline. I love cooking eggs in the leftover bacon magic! SERVES 4 • COOK TIME: 20 TO 25 MINUTES

1 (8-ounce) package bacon (check label for compliance if you're doing Whole30)

TERI'S TIPS

My oven runs hot, so I set it at 350°F. If your oven runs cooler, set it at 375°F. Watch the bacon and adjust the cooking time as needed.

Preheat the oven to 350°F. Line a baking sheet with parchment paper.

Spread the bacon slices over the lined baking sheet in a single layer. Bake for 20 to 25 minutes, or until the bacon reaches the crispiness you prefer. Remove the baking sheet from the oven and serve.

"Your best days are yet to come."   —*Unknown*

cooking techniques

Here are some cooking techniques every cook should know.

BLANCHING

I adore blanching as a way to retain the taste, texture, and color of vegetables, to keep them bright and crisp for salads, crudité platters, or stir-fries. Submerge vegetables briefly in boiling salted water to cook only the outermost layer. Pull them out with a slotted spoon and put them directly into a large bowl of ice water to shock them and stop the cooking. When cool, drain and dry them. My favorite vegetables to blanch are sugar snap peas (1 minute) and asparagus (2 minutes).

PARCOOKING

Parcooking goes a little bit further than blanching. I tend to parcook potatoes (5 to 15 minutes, depending on their type and size) and green beans (4 minutes). If you try to stir-fry them raw, they won't be cooked in the middle—parcooking gives them a head start. Also, parcooking works great with broccoli.

POACHING

Poaching is slowly simmering a food in seasoned liquid so the food cooks gently and gradually, while retaining its moisture. For bone-in, skin-on chicken breasts, I put an onion, a carrot, a stalk of celery, 1 tablespoon whole black peppercorns, and a good 2 tablespoons salt in a pot, add water, and bring it to a boil. Then I add the chicken breasts, which cool the water to a simmer the minute they're added, and poach them gently for about 25 minutes. Remove and let them cool. The poaching water makes a lovely stock. You'll find poached chicken in my egg roll (page 256) and chicken salad (page 97) recipes.

> **TERI'S TIPS**
> Cut down your prep time by parcooking vegetables and storing them in the fridge.
>
> Always parcook potatoes before adding them to frittatas or making potato crisps.

JUICING GINGER AND TURMERIC

I love fresh ginger and turmeric, but they can overwhelm a dish. Powdered can be very strong and chalky, so I developed an almost magical technique that uses the juice to infuse a gentle flavor.

Grate fresh, washed, unpeeled ginger or turmeric until you have about ¼ cup. Pick it up in your hands (see Tip), squeeze the juice into a

bowl, and discard the pulp. (Don't worry if you get a tiny bit of pulp in the juice.) Use the juice in recipes as needed. There is no substitute for fresh turmeric and ginger. They are such a boost to our health, because they infuse the food with so much life force.

TERI'S TIPS

I always use my bare hands to squeeze the juice, but turmeric does stain the hands temporarily, so feel free to wear gloves when squeezing the pulp.

index

NOTE: Page references in *italics* refer to photos of recipes.